FIRST NATIONS AVIATORS

T0359598

Compiled by

Squadron Leader Gary Oakley OAM and Group Captain John Martin

RAAF
HISTORY AND HERITAGE

The publishing of this book has been funded and managed by the History and Heritage Branch, Royal Australian Air Force.

All inquiries should be made to the publishers.
Big Sky Publishing Pty Ltd
PO Box 303, Newport, NSW 2106, Australia
Phone: 1300 364 611
Email: info@bigskypublishing.com.au
Web: www.bigskypublishing.com.au

Series: Australian Air Campaign Series; 4

A catalogue record for this book is available from the National Library of Australia

Cover design and typesetting by Think Productions, Melbourne

Front cover and title page: Flight Lieutenant Coomara Munro with the Queens Colour at Government House on 31 March 2021.

Acknowledgement

We pay our respects to the traditional custodians of this continent we call Australia. We acknowledge their elders, past and present. We also acknowledge all Aboriginal and Torres Strait Islander peoples, men and women, who have protected Country and Nation.

Warning

Aboriginal and Torres Strait Islander readers, please be advised that deceased people are represented throughout this publication.

Please be aware that any racist or derogatory language found in these accounts do not reflect the Royal Australian Air Force's or authors' viewpoint, rather the social attitudes and circumstances of the historical period in which they were created. Retaining it, however, helps us to better understand the lived experience of those times.

Terminology

The terms 'Indigenous', 'Aboriginal and Torres Strait Islander' and 'First Nations' are used interchangeably throughout this publication, reflecting the evolving preferences of those people who have gifted their stories to Air Force. In all other cases, these terms have been used respectfully to best support the narrative.

CONTENTS

FIRST NATIONS AVIATORS FOREWORD

We are delighted to provide the foreword to this, the first in a new series of official histories of the Royal Australian Air Force, focusing on Air Force people.

As the custodians of this land for more than 60,000 years, First Nations Peoples have been and will continue to watch over the land, seas and skies. Together as proud Australians, we all now share the responsibility of protecting Country. We acknowledge all Aboriginal and Torres Strait Islander peoples, and the men and women who have protected Country and Nation.

The Royal Australian Air Force's Centenary has provided us with an opportunity to reflect on the past 100 years. Importantly, this book is a poignant reminder of an all too often forgotten contribution made by our First Nations Peoples, and their endeavours and perseverance to protect this country, no matter the challenges.

First Nations Aviators provides that rare and brief glimpse into those Aboriginal and Torres Strait Islanders who have served in the Air Force since the Second World War in a variety of roles during wartime and in peace, some of whom, have paid the ultimate sacrifice for their country. Notwithstanding, all of those who have served, and who continue to serve, have made a commitment, regardless of the consequences, to uphold the security and safety of our country for the preservation of our sovereignty – you could not ask for any more.

Pleasingly, what this book does signify is a long and enduring relationship between First Nations Peoples and the Air Force, built on solid foundations of mutual trust and respect, long lasting friendships and positive legacies. Moreover, there is a real sense of changed perceptions and, with them, new opportunities and an ever-increasing endeavour to accept First Nations culture as an intrinsic part of Air Force operations.

What this book delivers is a brief and yet profound portrayal of those with an amazing resilience to protect Country and nation – we owe them and their families a huge debt of gratitude.

Robert Chipman AM CSC
Air Marshal
Chief of Air Force

Aunty Deb Booker
Air Force Elder

SERIES FOREWORD

The Australian Air Campaign Series produced by the Air Force's History and Heritage Branch will focus on four sub-series themed book titles:

- Campaigns, Operations and Battles,
- Capability and Technology,
- Bases and Airfields, and
- People

These themed titles are intended to explore specific facets of the Air Force from its inception in 1921. What they will reveal are unique insights, providing the reader with a greater appreciation and deeper understanding of those aspects that have shaped the Air Force's history and heritage.

Importantly, each of these publications will be sourced from official records and research, often including first-hand accounts. While these publications are endorsed for studies in military history, the range of topics will provide an ideal conduit for the broadest of audiences, to pursue and learn more about the many aspects that have contributed to the development of Australia's Air Force.

Apart from becoming a significant point of reference, these publications will ultimately acknowledge bravery, ingenuity, resilience – in essence, the service and sacrifice which is the hallmark of those who have served, and continue to serve, in the Air Force.

Robert Lawson OAM
Air Commodore
Director General History and Heritage – Air Force

FOREWORD

I believe that many people are unaware of the contribution the Aboriginal and Torres Strait Islander people make to serve their country. By enlisting and serving, they also took the opportunity to improve themselves, improve their communities, not only just for themselves but also for future generations to follow.

This book shows the commitment the First Nations Peoples have in defending Country, serving before they were legally allowed and proud of their service. We continue to serve today in the same tradition.

Harold (Harry) James Allie BEM
Inaugural Air Force Elder

INTRODUCTION

The decision to draw on the Air Force's Oral History Program to help create a series of books about people who have served, or continue to serve, in the Air Force is largely overdue.

I have had the privilege of being able to access our Oral History archives from the First World War through to current times and, on occasion, record or document personal stories for inclusion in our archives. Every story has a place in our collection and these stories deserve to be shared with a far broader audience. These publications will endeavour to make that happen.

Significantly, all stories offer an important conduit into our past and, in this case, a truly unique insight into the service of First Nations Peoples during times of peace and war. By telling their stories, we acknowledge their service and sacrifice and add a new chapter, which has long been missing, to our official histories.

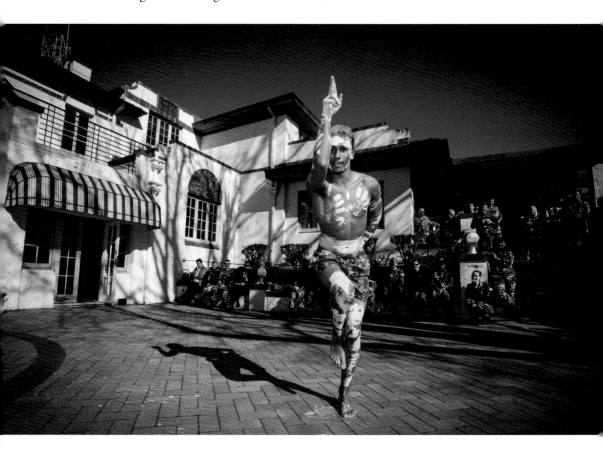

Working on this publication has highlighted the extent to which First Nations Peoples have actively served in Australia's military forces, including those before Federation. I was certainly surprised to find out how many First Nations Peoples had joined the Air Force during the Second World War. Squadron Leader Gary Oakley, a Gundungurra man from the Blue Mountains of New South Wales, our specialist First Nations advisor, has been central to this publication, and insisted, like many Australians, that I need not take these perceptions to heart because they were a product of what I was taught or told, or not told.

In our inaugural publication, *First Nations Aviators*, we have been gifted a number of stories from men and women who have proudly served and continue to serve the Air Force in various capacities, from the Second World War to today.

Albeit brief snapshots of each individual, for those who served during the Second World War, their service and sacrifice is especially admirable. The Defence Act 1903, until 1949, effectively banned their service based on race. However, even though First Nations Peoples were 'exempt' from serving, they answered the call to defend Country and served in two world wars.

Thankfully, things have improved since then and our Indigenous Liaison Officers (some of whom are featured in this publication), positioned on various Air Force bases, are testament to those improvements and the integral part played by First Nations Peoples in the Air Force.

Importantly, these stories should help to further acknowledge First Nations Peoples for the heroes they are and, in many cases, the recognition their families are due.

I could not think of a better way to introduce the Oral History series than by starting with *First Nations Aviators*, the very people who have been protecting this land and its interests for more than 60,000 years.

John Martin
Group Captain
Head – Air Force Oral History Program

HAROLD (HARRY) JAMES ALLIE BEM

Service Number: A113088
Date of Birth: 2 December 1942
Place of Birth: Charters Towers, Queensland
Date of Enlistment: 5 January 1966
Place of Enlistment: Charters Towers, Queensland
Date of Discharge: 12 July 1989
Rank: Warrant Officer

Above: No 482 Squadron 'Equipos' in the early 1970s. (RAAF)

Opposite top: Indigenous Veterans Commemoration. (Salty Dingo via RSL NSW)

Opposite bottom: Uncle Harry Allie at East Sale. (Harry Allie)

I was born in Charters Towers, a descendant of the Gudjala people. For my first 18 years I grew up in the town as there was a very large Aboriginal community in the area. I was always aware of things, particularly with our people. I was very fortunate. The pastoral industry in the region I grew up in was very large; this meant a lot of our people had work on cattle stations. At the time, many of my people were under the *Aboriginal Protection Act*. Being under the Act meant they were only allowed into town twice a year, which was at Christmas time for four weeks and the annual show around the end of June for two weeks. After their time in town, they went back to the stations. My family were never placed under the *Protection Act*, but we socialised and interacted with people that were and we saw the many hardships they faced.

The town of Charters Towers always had a strong military connection; this was instrumental to me wanting to enlist. However, it was my uncles and aunts, who served during the Second World War, who provided the strongest inspiration for me to join the Air Force.

My family and mob were very proud I had enlisted, even though it involved leaving my community. My previous life experiences placed me in good stead for service life and, in particular, a good understanding of discipline.

One of my favourite postings was at RAAF Base Butterworth in Malaysia and one of my most memorable times, during my service, was being sent to Sacramento, in the USA, to support the F-111C delivery to Australia.

Above: Warrant Officer Harry Allie receiving his Defence Force Service Medal in Malaysia. (Harry Allie)
Opposite bottom: The ferry team for the F-111s at Edwards Air Force Base. (Harry Allie)

66 *The strong help the weak and also the weak help the strong.* 99

After 23 years' service, I felt it was time to retire and I discharged in 1989. I now spend my time participating on boards and committees at the local, state and federal level. I can look back on my service and say it lived up to my expectations in many ways, particularly the equality which was given to me, the mateships I have formed and the many wonderful memories I now have. My time in the Air Force, the training, work experiences and postings have put me in good stead for the roles I have undertaken since discharging. I am particularly proud to have had the opportunity to serve my country as a First Nations person.

I believe that many people are unaware of the contribution the Aboriginal and Torres Strait Islander people make to serve their country. By enlisting and serving, they also took the opportunity to improve themselves, improve their communities, not only just for themselves but also for future generations to follow. This book shows the commitment the First Nations Peoples have in defending country, serving before they were legally allowed and proud of their service. We continue to serve today in the same tradition.

IVY EDITH MYRTLE BELL

Service Number: 94524
Date of Birth: 14 June 1910
Place of Birth: Arrino, Western Australia
Date of Enlistment: 30 November 1941
Place of Enlistment: Perth, Western Australia
Date of Discharge: 10 April 1946
Rank: Sergeant
Campaign: Second World War

Ivy Bell was born in Arrino, Western Australia, in 1910 and was employed as a cook for more than 17 years prior to enlisting in the Women's Auxiliary Australian Air Force (WAAAF). After Australia entered the Second World War, she registered in the Women's Voluntary National Register and, on 16 August 1941, applied to join the WAAAF. She then passed the Cooks trade test, displaying an all-round knowledge of cooking. Ivy enlisted as an aircraftwoman 1 at No 4 Recruit Centre, Perth, on 30 November 1941 where, as was the case for all WAAAFs, she declared her willingness to enlist for 'the period of the time of war now current and twelve months thereafter'. Ivy was 31 years old at the time.

Ivy attended No 1 School of Technical Training (1STT) in Melbourne where she completed No 56 Trainee Cooks Course and then completed No 26 Recruit Drill Course in March 1942. The school was formed as the Training Centre Barracks in 1939 at the old Melbourne Junior Technical School, West Melbourne, as a sub-unit of the Training Depot. It was renamed 1STT the following year to provide trade training for wireless/telegraphy operators, electricians, instrument makers and repairers, fitters, cooks, X-ray technicians, welders, mess stewards and high frequency radio

Above: Enlistment photo of Ivy Bell. (National Archives of Australia)

Opposite: Women of the WAAAF marching to St Paul's Cathedral, Victoria. (State Library Victoria, Argus Collection)

direction finding personnel. Several other courses were added in later years. Training was undertaken at several institutions including the Brunswick Technical College, the Amalgamated Wireless (Australia) School, the Footscray Technical College and the Emily McPherson School of Domestic Economy. With inadequate facilities, and overcrowding, the unit moved to the Exhibition Building in Carlton in March 1941, although a detachment remained behind until the facilities occupied by them were transferred to WAAAF trainees in October 1941. By the time the school disbanded on 22 December 1945, 21,324 trainees had graduated from 1STT.

With the exception of the time spent under training at 1STT in Melbourne, Ivy spent all of her service career in Western Australia. She was initially posted to Headquarters RAAF Station Pearce, located at Bullsbrook near Perth, and in May 1943 was posted to No 4 Aircraft Depot (4AD). Initially formed at Pearce on 15 May 1942, 4AD carried out the complete overhaul of engines, airframes and ancillary aircraft equipment. The depot relocated to RAAF Station Boulder two months after formation. This was a wartime military airfield established on the Boulder Racecourse between the twin towns of Kalgoorlie and Boulder, 600 kilometres east of Perth in the goldfields desert country. By November 1942, 4AD commenced engine overhauls of Pratt & Whitney R-1830 Twin Wasp engines, as used by RAAF Boomerangs, Beauforts, Catalinas and Dakotas (and, later for the RAAF, Liberator heavy bombers), which was to be a high priority task for the next three years. In the same month, the depot commenced work on its first aircraft, the Brewster Buffalos of No 25 Squadron. It began servicing No 14 Squadron Beauforts, also based at Pearce, in January 1943. The number of personnel on strength at 4AD exceeded 800 by late 1943.

With the end of the war approaching, Ivy was posted to No 4 Recruit Depot at Pearce. This unit conducted recruit drill and basic discipline courses. Ivy's final posting was to No 5 Personnel Depot in Subiaco, a suburb of Perth, from 10 October 1945. The depot's name had changed from No 5 Embarkation Depot in April 1944. At the end of September 1946, sections of the depot were established at Pearce, ANA House in Perth, and Karrakatta, to carry out discharge and recruiting duties. It ceased to function as a unit on 25 September and commenced disbandment.

Having joined the WAAAF as an aircraftwoman 1, Ivy was quickly promoted to temporary corporal on 1 December 1942 and temporary sergeant a year later. Sergeant Ivy Bell discharged from the WAAAF on 10 April 1946 and returned home to Moora, Western Australia.

Above: Aerial photo of RAAF Base Pearce. (RAAF)

Opposite top left: An RAAF cook (centre) explaining various cuts of meat to WAAAF trainee cooks during their course at No 1 School of Technical Training RAAF where Ivy attended. (RAAF)

Opposite top right: WAAAF cooks, 1943. (State Library NSW FL9571962)

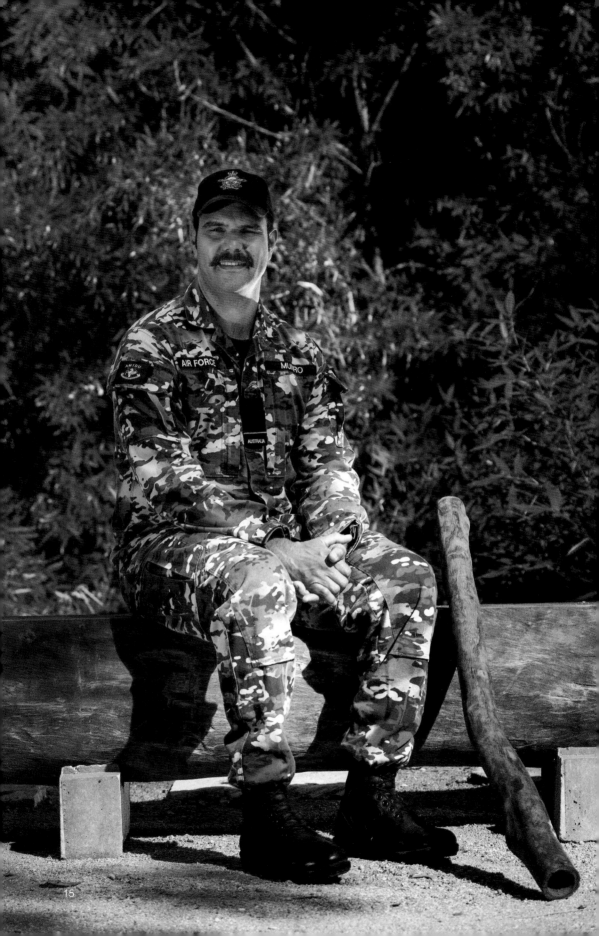

COOMARA MUNRO

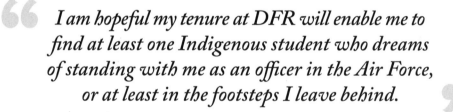

Date of Birth: 1 March 1984
Place of Birth: Tamworth, New South Wales
Date of Enlistment: 4 March 2003
Rank: Flight Lieutenant

> *I am hopeful my tenure at DFR will enable me to find at least one Indigenous student who dreams of standing with me as an officer in the Air Force, or at least in the footsteps I leave behind.*

I am a descendant of the Gumbaynggirr peoples of the mid-north coast of New South Wales. I also have close family ties to the mob all the way up the Macleay Valley from South West Rocks, through to Armidale and across to Tingha, New South Wales, which incorporates the Dunghutti, Anaiwan and Kamilaroi peoples.

My family has a very long and proud history serving with the Australian Defence Force (ADF). My mother, Liza Jane Munro, briefly served in the RAAF back in the early 1980s as a Steward. She met my father in the RAAF, a non-indigenous man who was an Aircraft Technician. He reached the rank of sergeant before discharging. Growing up, my grandmother would frequently remind me of my mother's brief history of service in the RAAF. She would tell me how proud she and my grandfather felt when Mum returned home to Tamworth after graduating recruit training at RAAF Edinburgh in South Australia.

My grandfather's two sisters, Gwendoline Munro and Wilga Williams (nee Munro) served in the Women's Royal Australian Air Force (WRAAF). As a young child, I remember visiting my great-grandmother's place in Tamworth, where she would remind me of my family history relating to their service. I remember asking myself, 'Surely serving in the Air Force is something I can do too?' My Aunty Wilga joined the WRAAF

Opposite: Personnel Capability Officer Flying Officer Coomara Munro, from Air Mobility Training and Development Unit, at the yarn circle on RAAF Base Richmond. (RAAF)

after my Aunty Gwendoline; I guess it was a case of the youngest sister following the eldest sister's lead. Interestingly, long after my Aunty Wilga left the WRAAF she was part of the famous 'Harry Williams and The Country Outcasts' (Koori Country Music band that toured Australia from the 1960s to the 1980s). Moreover, I think their stories of service played a pivotal role in my mother's decision to serve.

My great uncle, Private Frank Richard Archibald, also served and paid the ultimate sacrifice during the Second World War. He was born on 17 February 1915 in Walcha, New South Wales, the son of Frank and Sarah Archibald. Frank was the eldest son of 13 children and elected successor of the Gumbaynggirr peoples, whose lands stretch along the Pacific coast from the Nambucca River in the south to around the Clarence River in the north and the Great Dividing Range in the west. Frank lived in the Armidale– Walcha area until 1935, when the family moved to Burnt Bridge Mission, near Kempsey. The family had reportedly moved to the mission after authorities threatened to remove their children. Government authorities promised that their children would not be taken if the family moved to the mission.

Frank enlisted in the Australian Imperial Force at Kempsey in May 1940. He was assigned to reinforcements to the 2/2nd Infantry Battalion, part of the 16th Brigade within the 6th Division. His younger brother, Ronald, and his uncle, Richard, enlisted around the same time.

After some training at Greta, a small town in the Hunter Region, Frank was granted pre-embarkation leave in August before embarking at Sydney for overseas service. Arriving in Palestine in September, training continued until the 2/2nd Battalion advanced from Egypt into eastern Libya in January and February 1941. Frank and his comrades were then involved in the attacks to capture Bardia and Tobruk and remained as part of the Tobruk garrison as the advance continued. The 2/2nd left Tobruk, arriving in Greece in late March. Deployed north to resist the anticipated German invasion, a succession of Allied withdrawals meant the battalion did not meet the enemy in battle until 18 April. In a desperate fight, the 2/2nd blocked German movement to permit the safe withdrawal of Allied forces further south, holding its ground until overwhelmed by vastly superior German forces. During the evacuation, Frank was reportedly in a group of 12 cut off by the Germans. The group made its way to the coast where they obtained a fishing boat which took them to Crete.

In March 1942, Frank and the men of his battalion began making their way home. Arriving in Melbourne on 4 August 1942, a few weeks later Frank, known by his mates as 'Dickie', was welcomed back to Kempsey by his community at a public function.

After this brief trip home, Frank arrived at Port Moresby on 21 September 1942. His battalion fought major engagements at Templeton's Crossing, Oivi, and on the Sanananda Track, suffering heavy casualties in the process. Having started the campaign with almost 700 personnel, by the time the battalion fought its final actions in December

Above: Flying Officer Coomara Munro with Indigenous artist of the Darug Custodian Aboriginal Corporation (Windsor) Ms Leanne Watson at the Air Mobility Training and Development Unit. (RAAF)

1942, it had an effective strength of below 100, with many having been evacuated due to sickness. Frank's brother Ronald had become ill with malaria and was evacuated, but Frank continued, noting in his letters about how he used his bush skills to help fellow soldiers collect drinking water.

On 24 November 1942, the battalion was in the process of securing Sanananda when they encountered a group of Japanese soldiers dug in along the track. Under intense fire, the commander made the decision to split the platoon, leaving one group to engage the enemy while the rest moved forward. Frank was with the group engaging the enemy when he noticed a friend caught in a dangerous position; as he was trying to save his friend, he was shot and killed. He was 27 years old. Initially buried near where he fell, his remains were later reinterred in Port Moresby (Bomana) War Cemetery.

On Anzac Day 2012, members of the Archibald family gathered at the cemetery to call Frank's spirit home in a traditional spiritual ceremony. Soil was also taken from his gravesite and reinterred with his family in Armidale Cemetery. His name is also listed on the Roll of Honour at the Australian War Memorial, Canberra.

It was now my turn to serve. I enlisted in the RAAF as an Airfield Defence Guard (Active Reservist) in March 2003 and was posted to Nos 1 and 3 Security Forces Squadrons (formerly Nos 1 and 3 Airfield Defence Squadron detachments at RAAF Amberley and RAAF Edinburgh respectively), spending the next few years attending regular training and domestic exercises. This involved returning home at monthly intervals. I was so proud to be able to share my experiences with family of life 'living and working' in the bush while on exercise.

In 2005, as a reservist, I deployed on what was my first operation to the Middle East (Operations *Catalyst* and *Slipper*) for four months in support of airbase security operations. When I returned, the opportunity to sign a Permanent Air Force contract arose and I jumped at the chance. In 2006, I deployed to Timor-Leste on Operation *Astute* for three months and again assisted with the maintenance of airbase security operations.

For the next six years I had a number of postings and also deployed to Pakistan on Operation *Pakistan Assist II* which was a humanitarian operation after the 2010 floods in that country. I participated in aircraft security exercises in both RMAF Butterworth, Malaysia, and Andersen Air Force Base, USAF, Guam. It was an amazing experience working alongside the USAF, as it was there that I really started to appreciate the taste of beef jerky and proper American-style sandwiches. I was also deployed locally to south-east Queensland during Operation *Queensland Flood Assist*, helping the locals with clean-up efforts after the 2011 floods.

Through my posting to Defence Force Recruiting (DFR), Canberra, as a Careers Counsellor, I started believing I could become an officer in the Air Force. I was promoted to sergeant and posted to RAAF Base Wagga, New South Wales, as a training team supervisor and instructor. This was very rewarding as it felt as though I had come 'full circle' in my Air Force career, especially seeing my recruit photo on the wall in the classroom hallway. It was exciting to meet people I recruited from my time at Defence Force Recruiting, particularly when the graduating trainees would openly thank me for helping them realise their dreams of joining the Air Force.

I finally applied for a commission in 2017 and, in 2018, I was sent to Officer Training School (OTS) as a Ground Defence Officer Trainee and received a Silver Commendation for building teamwork and demonstrating RAAF values, and was the recipient of the course physical training award. Thereafter, I posted to the Royal Military College Duntroon, spending eight months there as a cadet before re-specialising to Personnel Capability Officer (PCO) in June 2019. After completing this training, I was posted to the Air Mobility Training and Development Unit, RAAF Richmond, as a PCO. This was where I continued to develop my core skills as a junior PCO, unit administrator and welfare support officer. In 2020, I was deployed on Operation *COVID-19 Assist* for three months. I am now the Senior Careers Coach and Careers Promotion Team Leader for the Defence Force Recruiting Centre, Rhodes, New South Wales. Responsibilities include working with a team of Career Coaches to promote ADF careers by giving presentations, interviews, answering questions and discussing service life formally and informally with ADF candidates.

I am hopeful my tenure at DFR will enable me to find at least one Indigenous student who dreams of standing with me as an officer in the Air Force, or at least in the footsteps I leave behind.

Without a doubt, my career highlight to date was performing the role of Queen's Colour Bearer (New) for the Air Force 2021 Centenary Parade because it was a tremendous honour to acknowledge and pay respect to our Air Force history and culture. Especially so, it was an opportunity to stand for those Indigenous veterans who have also served and who themselves would not have otherwise had that same opportunity to stand before His Excellency, The Governor-General of Australia. I remember asking my grandmother once 'What does it really mean to be Aboriginal?' Her response was that it is about survival and knowing who you are and where you're going. This is another reason why it was so special for me to be selected as the Queen's Colour Bearer for Air Force. The occasion was most certainly symbolic of who we are as an organisation, where we've been and our shared love and respect for our past, present and future.

One of the most rewarding things about my time in the Air Force is that on many occasions there have been leaders who have looked beyond my ethnicity, including me and empowering me to be a leader also. I am so very blessed to be counted among these great people and look forward to further opportunities to encourage and support others for the same reasons.

> *I remember asking my grandmother once 'What does it really mean to be Aboriginal?' Her response was that it is about survival and knowing who you are and where you're going.*

Left: Queen's Colour Bearer Flying Officer Coomara Munro with the new Queen's Colour at Government House in Canberra to commemorate the centenary of the Royal Australian Air Force. (RAAF)

Right: The Governor-General of the Commonwealth of Australia, His Excellency General the Honourable David Hurley AC DSC (Retd), returns the newly consecrated Queen's Colour to the new Queen's Colour bearer, Flying Officer Coomara Munro during the Queen's Colour Parade held at Government House, Canberra. (RAAF)

AGNES MAUDE BONNEY

Service Number: 114375
Date of Birth: 7 February 1925
Place of Birth: Bordertown, South Australia
Date of Enlistment: 8 May 1944
Place of Enlistment: Adelaide, South Australia
Date of Discharge: 15 January 1946
Rank: Aircraftwoman 1
Campaign: Second World War

Above: Women waiting for processing into the WAAAF. (John Oxley Library, State Library of Queensland)
Opposite: Enlistment photo of Agnes Bonney. (National Archives of Australia)

Agnes Bonney was born in early 1925 in Bordertown, South Australia. On 8 May 1944, aged 19, the neat and quietly spoken young lady presented at No 5 Recruiting Centre (5RC) in Adelaide and enlisted in the Women's Auxiliary Australian Air Force (WAAAF) as a Stewardess with the rank of aircraftwoman 1. In her enlistment papers, Agnes had noted her civilian occupation as a waitress. It was a busy time. Agnes was one of 71 ground staff enlisted at 5RC that day. She was also one of 262 RAAF and 56 WAAAF members enlisted during the month. Although she was 19, Agnes was authorised to draw the adult rate of pay.

Immediately after enlistment, she was posted to No 4 Initial Training School (4ITS) at Mount Breckan, Victor Harbour, South Australia. The school had formed on 4 November 1940 to train aircrew, while its WAAAF Training Centre commenced on 8 March 1942. Between those dates and its disbandment on 3 December 1944, 5,595 aircrew and 2,604 WAAAFs had graduated from courses at the school.

At 4ITS, Agnes was enrolled in No 79 Recruit Drill Course which commenced on 9 May 1944. She was one of 53 WAAAF recruits plus 245 other trainees inducted for training at 4ITS that month. As required by RAAF mobilisation orders, shortly after arriving at 4ITS, Agnes completed her will, appointing her mother, Edith Maude Bonney, who lived in Victoria, as executrix and sole beneficiary. The will was witnessed by two fellow students on the course, Hilda Butler and Madge May Appelkamp. In her enlistment papers, Agnes named her father, Thomas John Bonney of Kingston, South Australia, as her next of kin.

During Agnes's time at 4ITS, the Commanding Officer reported that WAAAF and aircrew training had proceeded smoothly and satisfactorily, and that good discipline was maintained both within and outside the station. Having successfully completed recruit and drill training in June 1944, Agnes was posted to No 1 WAAAF Depot to undertake Stewardess training. The depot had formed at Malvern, Victoria, on 6 May 1941. After several other moves, in January 1943 the depot's final move was to 'Larundel' in Bundoora (near Preston), Victoria, a facility which, post-war, was converted to a mental institution. The depot disbanded on 19 October 1945.

While at No 1 WAAAF Depot, Agnes successfully completed No 151 Mess Stewardess Course. She was then posted to the Adelaide Wireless Transmission Station from 9 July. At the time of her arrival, the station had a personnel strength of 189, which included five WAAAF officers and 114 WAAAF other ranks. The station frequently provided guards for American Liberator aircraft visiting Gawler. The Salvation Army and the Young Women's Christian Association added to the furnishings of the station's Recreation Hut, improving its amenity and comfort.

Erection of buildings and installation of equipment at the Adelaide Wireless Transmitting Station site had begun on 10 February 1942. Cypher and other operations commenced during March and, on 1 February 1945, the unit was renamed Gawler Telecommunications Unit. The unit operated an Operations Building, Remote Receiving Building and Transmitting Building at Gawler. Wireless telegraphists would work three daily shifts in an underground bunker. They would access the underground bunker via a small wooden building on a flat open area of the Gawler base. The unit was disbanded on 31 May 1946.

From Gawler, Agnes was posted on staff at No 1 Personnel Depot (1PD) in Melbourne on 31 August 1945. Hostilities in the Pacific had ceased 16 days earlier. At the time Agnes arrived at the depot, there were 11 WAAAF officers and 134 WAAAF other ranks on strength out of a total unit population of 621. The final entry in 1PD's unit history is dated 31 October 1945.

On 22 December 1945, Agnes was posted to No 1 Engineering School. At the time, the school was located in Ascot Vale, Victoria. However, in early March 1946, it relocated to RAAF Forest Hill (later RAAF Wagga), in New South Wales, where it eventually became the RAAF School of Technical Training, a currently active RAAF school.

Aircraftwoman Agnes Bonney posted from No 1 Engineering School, reporting to No 1 Personnel Depot where she completed her discharge on 11 February 1946. In the later stages of her career, she was twice recommended as suitable for promotion.

Above left: Gawler Telecommunication unit RAAF facility, South Australia. (State Library of South Australia)
Above right: A WAAAF Cook and Mess Steward pose for recruiting photos. (State Library of South Australia)
Opposite: Gawler Telecommunications Unit. (State Library of South Australia)

CLIVE JOSEPH ROBIN BRYANT

Service Number:	A224174
Date of Birth:	5 July 1947
Place of Birth:	Bellingen, New South Wales
Date of Enlistment:	1967
Date of Discharge:	1973
Rank:	Leading Aircraftman
Campaign:	Vietnam

" *When I put the uniform on, I represent Australia and I represent my contribution to Australia.* "

Clive was born in 1947 on Gumbaynggir country the country of his mothers people. His father was a Walbanga man from the south coast of New South Wales. As a child, he grew up in Bellwood, Nambucca Heads, and was educated at Bellwood Public School. In 1959, he was taken to Darlington, Sydney, along with his younger sister for further education and employment opportunities. He finished schooling and gained his High School Certificate.

Above: No 9 Squadron UH-1H Iroquois A2-773 call sign *'Bushranger'* banks as an RAAF Door gunner fires his twin M60 machine guns at enemy positions. (RAAF)

Opposite: Clive Bryant at the Amberley Heritage Centre. (Clive Bryant)

Clive's sister had married a member of the RAAF. Clive would often take trips out to RAAF Base Richmond just to look at the aircraft. In 1967, Clive decided to join the RAAF, doing his recruit training at RAAF Bases Edinburgh and Wagga where he learned engineering and qualified as an airframe fitter.

As an Airframes Mechanic, he was posted to No 5 Squadron, RAAF Base Fairbairn, Canberra, to work on Iroquois helicopters. Clive was posted to Wagga to do his fitters course and, on completion, was posted back to Canberra. In April 1970, he was posted to No 9 Squadron at Vung Tau in Vietnam. Clive was one of three First Nations RAAF members posted to Vung Tau at the time. He completed a 12-month tour of duty in Vietnam and was then posted to No 36 Squadron at RAAF Base Richmond. He discharged from the RAAF as a leading aircraftman in 1973.

On leaving the Air Force, Clive completed a Bachelor of Business at Ku-ring-gai College in 1988. He has been involved in several Indigenous businesses ranging from rehabilitation centres to the performing arts. Active in the economic development of Aboriginal and Torres Strait Islander people in small business, he is also involved in Native Title and on the board of Gaagal Wanggaan South Beach National Park.

Clive lives back on the land of his mother, having purchased the original property on the land where he was born and brought up.

Above: A No 9 Squadron RAAF UH-1H Iroquois undergoing repairs to replace a tail boom. (AVM Donald Tidd AM MBE)

Opposite: Members of No 9 Squadron, Vung Tau, Vietnam, Date Circa 1971. (RAAF)

It is most important that Aboriginal and Torres Strait Islander peoples can celebrate on their own terms the lives of their brothers, sisters, parents, grandparents and great-grandparents in whichever theatre of war they served.

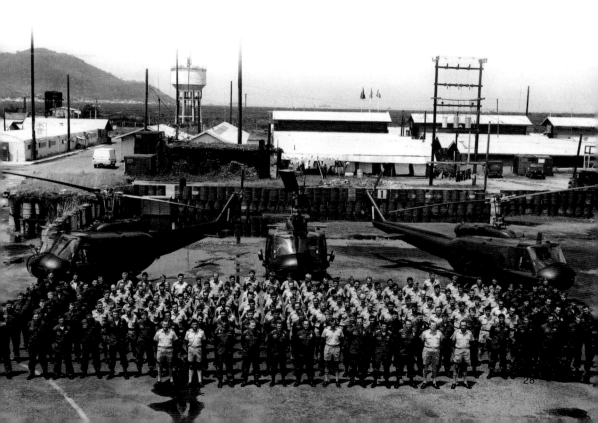

VINCENT DOUGLAS BUNDA

Service Number: A1714 and 172096
Date of Birth: 16 September 1922
Place of Birth: Cherbourg, Queensland
Date of Enlistment: 19 May 1947
Place of Enlistment: Brisbane, Queensland
Date of Discharge: 20 November 1975
Rank: Sergeant
Campaign: Second World War and Korea

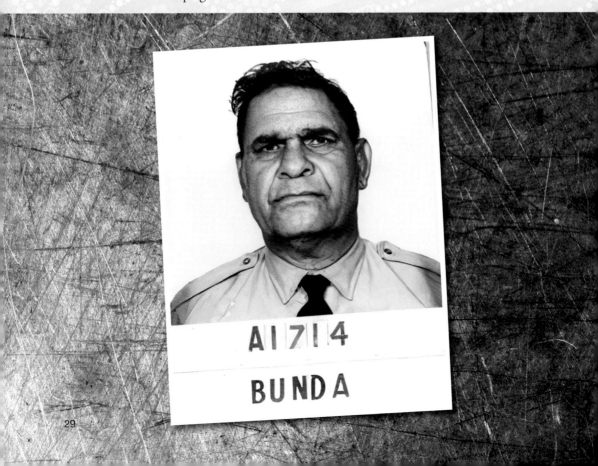

A1714

BUNDA

" *There's one simple way of describing life in the RAAF – colossal – and frankly I wouldn't want to change places with anyone.* "

Above: Empire Day Parade, British Commonwealth Occupation Force, Tokyo, circa 1949. (State Library Victoria, Argus Collection)

Opposite: Enlistment photo of Vince Bunda. (National Archives of Australia)

Vince was born on the Cherbourg Aboriginal Settlement, in Wakka Wakka country, Queensland, in 1922. Cherbourg was originally gazetted as a mission station in 1901, known as Barambah Industrial School, for the local First Nations peoples. However, Barambah became the receiving place for people from the South Burnett region and elsewhere under then government policy. In 1935, it was estimated there were 28 'tribal' groups present.

Originally joining the Army in 1942, Vince was one of 19 Cherbourg men to enlist during the Second World War. He served with the 2/3 Field Company, Royal Australian Engineers, in the Middle East, New Guinea and Borneo campaigns and was demobbed on 15 January 1946. He reached the rank of corporal during his Army service. Vince then became a full-time trainee carpenter under the Commonwealth Reconstruction Training Scheme.

Vince enlisted in the Interim Air Force as an Aircraftman Class 1 Carpenter General on 19 May 1947 in Brisbane. The Interim Air Force was a transitional force which existed in the immediate post-war period. Vince was posted to No 3 Aircraft Depot, RAAF Base Amberley, where he completed No 13 Recruit Drill Course, after which he was attached to No 60 Operational Base Unit at Morotai in the latter half of 1947. Morotai formed part of the aerial route to Japan where RAAF units operated as part of the British Commonwealth Occupation Force. During this attachment, Vince reclassified as a leading aircraftman.

On 30 September 1948, Vince enlisted in the Permanent Air Force, and, between January and November 1950, was posted to No 10 Squadron at Amberley. The unit was tasked with conducting maritime and anti-submarine patrols over northern Australia and the South Pacific. After arriving there, Vince was soon promoted to corporal, and, on 2 February 1951, he flew to Japan for a posting to No 391 (Base) Squadron. The squadron was based at Iwakuni and formed part of No 91 (Composite) Wing which also encompassed Nos 77 and 491 (Maintenance) Squadrons and No 30 Communications Flight.

On 25 June 1950, North Korea invaded South Korea. The Mustangs of No 77 Squadron engaged in combat operations soon after with the remaining units of No 91 Wing providing support. Vince's unit, No 391 Squadron, was responsible for a range of functions including administrative, logistical, medical, communications and security functions at Iwakuni, while also maintaining detachments in South Korea. It included a marine section for harbour patrols and search-and-rescue in the waters off southern Japan. While with the squadron, as a corporal, Vince was in charge of the carpenter's shop where his primary duties were general construction and carpentry – in essence, all aspects of woodwork and repair.

The RAAF's A Grade cricket team pictured in Kure, Japan, during the October 1952 competition. Vince Bunda third from left in the back row. (Australian War Memorial)

QX28558 CORPORAL
V. D. BUNDA
2/3 FIELD COMPANY R.A.E.
9TH JUNE 1986 AGE 62

SADLY MISSED BY HIS FAMILY

" *There is no doubt in my mind, the Air Force is a great life and it's the sort of thing I would strongly recommend to any ambitious, forward-looking young man.* "

Vince returned to Amberley in July 1952 and had brief postings to No 10 Squadron, Base Squadron Amberley and No 3 Aircraft Depot (3AD) before being posted to No 2 Airfield Construction Squadron at Momote, Manus Island, on 22 August 1953. The squadron was engaged in rehabilitating the airfield facilities on the island. Vince returned to Amberley and 3AD once more on 29 December 1954.

Between 1955 and 1971, Vince had postings to 3AD (multiple occasions), No 2 Stores Depot at Regents Park, New South Wales, and No 482 Squadron at Amberley. He was promoted to sergeant in 1971 while with 3AD. Between 1972 and 1974, he was posted to Base Squadron Butterworth in Malaysia. Vince returned to No 2 Stores Depot in 1975 and discharged from the RAAF later that year.

In addition to his Second World War medals, Vince was awarded the Korea Medal and the United Nations Service Medal for his time supporting the RAAF's operations during the Korean War.

Sergeant Vince Bunda discharged from the RAAF on 20 November 1975 after 28 years of service.

TRISH MACKINTOSH

Date of Birth: 23 March 1968
Place of Birth: Penrith, New South Wales
Date of Enlistment: 11 May 1989
Place of Enlistment: Townsville, Queensland
Rank: Warrant Officer

66
… I was the first female of my family,
in history, to join the ADF.
99

My family are very proud descendants of the Tubba-Gah clan of the Wiradjuri Nation in New South Wales. I spent my early years growing up visiting Dubbo often and I maintain a strong connection with the area visiting family and extended family members who still reside on Country; my mother, Narrell Boys (née Peckham), is an active Elder.

My initial interest in the Air Force came after a recruiting team visited my school in Mareeba in Far North Queensland. However, four years would pass before a career in the Air Force would become a serious consideration and realisation. Over those four years, I studied at a business college, and worked as a barmaid, kitchen hand, cleaner, teacher's aide, and governess and carer in Kowanyama, Cape York Peninsula. Going from job to job and not having any real career prospects, I looked back at the visit from the recruiting team and decided to join the Air Force.

As it happened, I accepted an offer of employment and joined the Air Force on 11 May 1989, quickly realising I was the first female member of my family, in history, to join the ADF. My grandmother's brother, James 'Jim' Burns, and other distant relatives were in the Army.

Opposite: Uncle Harry Allie and Trish Mackintosh at the 2017 NSW Aboriginal Remembrance Ceremony. (RAAF)

Dubbo Photo News April 27-May 3, 2017

21

DUBBO WEEKENDER

OPINION, ANALYSIS, FEATURES, DEPTH.

Wings of the Wiradjuri

There was once a time when Indigenous service men and women were denied official thanks or dues, despite laying their lives on the line for Australia. Fortunately, things have dramatically changed and the experience of visiting Australian Air Force Flight Sergeant Patricia Withers, a Tubbah-gar-Wiradjuri woman, has been a positive one, YVETTE AUBUSSON-FOLEY writes.

SHE'S served 27 years in the Air Force and is a decorated service woman, having seen active service in Iraq and Afghanistan.

The mum of two is also ninth generation Tubbah-gar-Wiradjuri and, although she's lived in many places around Australia and overseas, her roots are here in Dubbo where her mother Narell Boys and aunty Coral Peckham are proud beyond words to see one of their own, Flight Sergeant Patricia Withers, march for the first time in Dubbo's Anzac Parade.

"I remember when she graduated as a rookie. She was marching straight toward me and the tears were streaming down her face, and mine," Narell said.

It was a shared joke on the Monday before Anzac Day, warning each other to not make eye contact at the service in case it triggered too much emotion the proud Wiradjuri women all knew they'd be feeling.

"It's the first time I've marched in Dubbo or even been with family on Anzac Day. I could have stayed in Melbourne or gone to Canberra but really felt the need to come here this year. I have a lot of family here, mum, aunties. This is where my roots are," Patricia told Dubbo Photo News.

She had to apply for permission to be here then discuss her plans with the local RSL.

Patricia first considered the Air Force as a career option when she was at school in Mareeba, in the Atherton Tablelands, west of Cairns.

"I finally decided to join in 1989 so I went to recruitment to sign up but they said it would take about 18 months. I needed to get out of that town and begged them for anything so they found a position and in two weeks I was on my way. Normally, a letter would follow recruitment with instructions on what to pack and what to wear.

"I hadn't seen the letter so I turned up in jeans and T-shirt and my hair was out everywhere. They were like, 'Oh!', so they found me a hairband and tidied me up."

These days she looks pristine in her dress uniform.

"On May 11, it will be my 28th year," Patricia said.

Twenty-one of those years have been served in Darwin and the Northern Territory at the RAAF Base Tindal until a more recent move to Melbourne.

On Friday, May 26, Patricia will be a guest speaker at the Aboriginal and Torres Strait Islander Veterans Commemoration Service in Sydney, a National Reconciliation Week event held at the Pool of Reflection at the Anzac Memorial.

"Coming home helps me learn about my history. I want to know it. I want to show that women can have a career and a family and travel with the Air Force," she said.

Patricia has two children, Tiarna, 18, and Taine, 10. "Although I am divorced the Air Force remains supportive."

Sitting in on our interview, it's very clear Patricia has abundant family support too.

"She's the first woman in our family to join the air force," boasts aunt Coral, who arranged a busload of friends and family to support Patricia on Anzac Day and share lunch and a bit of Two-Up.

"I'm the Two-Up Queen, I love it," Patricia laughed, patting the blue pockets of her uniform jacket, "I've got deep pockets. I've got my 'in' pocket and my 'out' pocket."

At 49, she has just 11 years until retirement after which she plans to open a café, but is likely to end up mentoring young women and men, perhaps here in Dubbo.

Her passion for travel has been satisfied by the Air Force. She loves Dubai and found working in the Middle East put her in close proximity to many different types of aircraft, although she backed out of the chance to sit in a fighter jet, put off by the unusual breathing required under G-forces.

"I recall one time a group of us were strapped in to the back of a Caribou with the back door open and we sat on the edge of the back door with our legs dangling over the edge, flying over Katherine. It was fantastic. I've had many fantastic experiences," she said.

Significantly, she is now part of the mentoring program for other women joining the Air Force, particularly indigenous women, and an incredibly important role for a Wiradjuri woman coming to terms with the importance matriarchal ties

have in the Wiradjuri nation.

Patricia's shining medals tell the story of her Air Force family, of her long service and active duty tours to two of the most dangerous war zones on Earth; Afghanistan in 2008 and Iraq in 2005.

Employed in logistics, even Patricia's mum Narell wasn't allowed to know where her daughter was serving. "It was a need to know only basis, I was told," she said.

> **I recall one time a group of us were strapped in to the back of a Caribou with the back door open and we sat on the edge of the back door with our legs dangling over the edge, flying over Katherine. It was fantastic. I've had many fantastic experiences.**

Flight Sergeant Patricia Withers who participated in the Dubbo Anzac Parade this week.

Flight Sergeant Patricia Withers with her son Taine, 10, and aunt Coral Peckham (left) and mother Narell Boys (right).

Dubbo Weekender – 'Wings of the Wiradjuri'. (RAAF)

After taking up employment in the Equipment Account and Supply trades, apart from some short postings to Air Force bases near Newcastle in New South Wales and Laverton in Victoria, I would spend the majority of my time working between the Northern Territory's Air Force bases at Tindal and Darwin. My work would touch on air movements, stores accounting, stock control and procurement activities for both Base Support and Expeditionary Units and also the Air Force's prestigious No 75 Squadron that operated the F/A-18 Hornet at Tindal.

In addition to my time in Australia, I have deployed to the Middle East on three occasions and additionally to Asia in support of fighter operations. While these deployments have provided me with unforgettable experiences, I would be quick to add I have witnessed a lot of cool stuff but, unfortunately, you can't take pictures for security reasons to prove it.

Although my earlier intentions were to advance through the ranks and develop relevant managerial skills to take with me to use in civilian life, I found myself enjoying my Air Force career enough to stay on. I never thought I would become a 'lifer', but the years burned quickly as I had job satisfaction, promotions and employment security.

Today, I am working at Headquarters Air Command in Glenbrook, New South Wales, as the Air Command Warrant Officer for Indigenous Affairs. In this role, I provide specialist advice and assistance to the Senior Leadership Team, the Indigenous Liaison Officer network located on various Air Force bases across Australia, and those senior and junior enlisted Indigenous personnel currently serving in the Air Force. My aims are to promote cultural awareness with non-Indigenous and Indigenous Air Force members and promote those youth programs that would give Indigenous youth a taste of life in the Air Force.

'I never thought I would become a "lifer", but the years burned quickly as I had job satisfaction, promotions and employment security.'

BRADLEY ISHIGUCHI

Date of Birth: 12 October 1992
Place of Birth: Derby, Western Australia
Date of Enlistment: 24 May 2011
Place of Enlistment: Townsville, Queensland
Rank: Pilot Officer

> *Being able to remain in the Air Force Reserves has meant I have been able to continue to serve my country.*

I was born in Derby, Western Australia, and I am a part of the Nyikina mob who are an Aboriginal people from the Kimberley region. My heritage is Aboriginal, Japanese and English, with the Aboriginal line coming from a union between my great-grandfather, a Japanese deep-sea diver, and my great-grandmother of Aboriginal descent. My mother came from England as a 'ten-pound pom', a scheme going back to the 1960s that encouraged British people to sail from the UK to start a new life in Australia for ten pounds.

I grew up in Derby until I was about ten years old. My father worked as a Fly In, Fly Out, 'Jumbo' drill operator in an underground mine located outside of Fitzroy Crossing. In 2002, my father was offered a job in Townsville at the Cannington Mine, so we all moved. I completed the remainder of my primary and secondary schooling in Townsville. I had always had a keen interest in aviation and flying and set about getting my unrestricted pilot's licence. At the same time, I joined the Air Force Cadets in Townsville. Then, as soon as I was old enough, I combined these interests and joined the Air Force in 2011.

On joining the Air Force, I became a Movements Operator, also known as a 'Mover', which is an essential element of the ground crew and airfield logistics team, responsible for efficiently moving all manner of personnel, equipment and supplies.

Opposite and above: Bradley on his driver training course in the Mount Kosciuszko National Park, 2012. (Bradley Ishiguchi)

In my time as a Mover, I enjoyed the manifesting and weight and balancing activities associated with the likes of C-130 and C-17 aircraft, and achieving various vehicle licences, including truck and forklift. I have also become involved in the testing, dispensing and quality control of aviation fuels. As a Mover I gained an incredible amount of knowledge and experience that would prove valuable in the future.

I have been posted to a variety of locations, including Darwin to work with their Air Movements Section. I have also completed several deployments, including to East Timor on Operation *Astute*, the Australian-led military deployment to quell unrest and return stability to East Timor, working with Australia's commandos in Papua New Guinea and the Papua New Guinea Defence Force. I have also served in Afghanistan on Operation *Slipper* and been a part of the team that prepared our F/A-18 Hornets for their deployment to the Middle East to fight ISIS as part of Operation *Okra*.

During my service, I have participated in some of the ADF's biggest regular exercises, including *Talisman Sabre*, where thousands of personnel from various nations participate in land, sea and air exercises, and Exercise *Pitch Black*, the RAAF's biennial air warfare exercise conducted between Darwin and Tindal comprising up to 100 aircraft from countries such as Australia, Singapore, Thailand, Malaysia, India, Canada and the US.

In 2018, I was accepted into a Qantas pilot program, so I transferred to the Reserves and, while my desire to become a Qantas pilot did not eventuate, at the end of 2019 I found myself back in Western Australia, working as a commercial pilot for North-West Bush Pilots. I finished with the Bush Pilots in mid-2020 and started working in youth mental health and suicide for an Aboriginal health service.

Being able to remain in the Air Force Reserves has meant I have been able to continue to serve my country. I have participated in the Air Force's Operation *COVID-19 Assist* and more recently with Indigenous Affairs. The big change in my life and my Air Force career happened in 2022. I was offered an undergraduate's position with the University of Western Sydney to study medicine and become an Air Force Medical Officer. I am looking forward to the next chapter of my life and the challenges that will surely come with it. The next chapter in my life has started.

> *The distance between the impossible and possible is merely measured by one's determination.*
> – Captain James Thain

Opposite, top and bottom: On operation in Tarin Kowt, Afghanistan, in 2013 as part of the Air Movements Team, Combat Support Unit. (Bradley Ishiguchi)

ALICE LOVETT

Service Number: 95994
Date of Birth: 16 June 1922
Place of Birth: Hamilton, Victoria
Date of Enlistment: 10 June 1942
Place of Enlistment: Melbourne, Victoria
Date of Discharge: 17 May 1943
Rank: Aircraftwoman
Campaign: Second World War

Born in the Southern Grampians town of Hamilton, in south-west Victoria, in mid-1922, Alice Lovett was living in Brighton, Victoria, when, one month short of her 20th birthday, she applied to join the Women's Auxiliary Australian Air Force (WAAAF). The Lovett family has a long tradition of service in the Services from the First World War to after the Second World War. Alice's personnel file shows that at least two other members of the family served in the RAAF during the 1940s, though it is unknown exactly what their relationship was to Alice. They are Leading Aircraftman Robert Leonard Lovett, who served in the South-West Pacific, and Flying Officer John Edward Lovett who served in the United Kingdom and Canada.

Extending the family tradition, Alice, a diminutive five feet (1.52 metres) tall, lodged her application at No 1 Recruiting Centre to enrol in the WAAAF, for a period not exceeding 12 months, in early May 1942. She applied to join the Messwoman mustering and was employed as a domestic worker at the time.

The recruiting centre had opened on Latrobe Street in Melbourne on 17 September 1939, just two weeks after the declaration of war in Europe. By May 1942, having moved three times, it was located in the Preston Motors Building in Melbourne. The recruitment of WAAAFs commenced in April 1941. Recruitment efforts accelerated after the commencement of war in the Pacific in December 1941. In May 1942, No

Informal group portrait Aircraftwoman Alice Lovett, a member of the Women's Auxiliary Australian Air Force and two civilian friends, Mary King (left), and Eileen Watson. (Australian War Memorial)

1 Recruiting Centre enlisted 2,822 personnel, of whom 411 were WAAAFs. Having completed recruitment formalities, Alice enrolled in the WAAAF on 10 June 1942, six days before turning 20. In that month, she was one of 275 WAAAFs, out of a total of 2,216 new enlistees, to join up at the centre.

Alice was posted to No 1 Initial Training School to undertake the Recruit Drill Course. The school had formed in April 1940 to provide initial training for pilots, observers and air gunners as part of the Empire Air Training Scheme and was established on the Mornington Peninsula, in Victoria, at Lord Somers Camp with additional land from the Coolart estate acquired under the provisions of the National Security Regulations. The school occupied about 92.5 acres which gave it the required capacity to train 600 aircrew.

On 1 July 1941, the Women's Auxiliary in Somers started a canteen service for No 1 Initial Training School. A newsletter called the *Somers Sun* was started to also help morale at the isolated camp. Regular sporting competitions in rugby union, tennis and cricket kept students occupied.

The first WAAAF trainees arrived in March 1942 and the first three WAAAF Recruit Drill Courses, Nos 1, 2 and 3, took place between 12 March and 9 April. Alice was one of 88 WAAAF recruits who reported to the school on 10 June 1942 and, on 7 July, she was one of a combined 72 WAAAFs who graduated from Nos 8, 9 and 10 Recruit Drill Courses. The population on the base at the time was about 1,400 RAAF and WAAAF personnel employed or under training. With the cessation of hostilities in Europe in May 1945, aircrew training ceased in June. The school completed disbandment on 19 October, less than two months after the official end of hostilities in the Pacific. After the war, the site was acquired again by the Commonwealth Government for use as a holding centre for migrant families. The Somers site is currently used as a school camp.

Having completed recruit training, Alice was posted to No 2 Air Navigation School at Nhill, Victoria, in July 1942. The school was initially raised at Mount Gambier in South Australia on 1 July 1941 but moved to Nhill in September that year. It initially provided celestial navigational training for air observers, but later increased its course offerings. When Alice arrived at the school there were 510 personnel on strength, 57 of whom were WAAAFs. The school eventually disbanded on 9 December 1943 after graduating 2,002 trainees.

Alice only served as a WAAAF Messwoman for 342 days before requesting discharge. She discharged at No 1 Embarkation Depot, which was located at the Melbourne Cricket Ground at the time.

Aircraftwoman Alice Lovett discharged at her own request on 17 May 1943.

Informal portrait of Aircraftwoman Alice Lovett (left) and her friend Mary King. (Australian War Memorial)

BRETT WEST

Date of Birth:	26 June 1969
Place of Birth:	Perth, Western Australia
Place of Enlistment:	Perth, Western Australia
Date of Enlistment:	9 March 1987
Rank:	Warrant Officer

'… I used to marvel at the small aircraft that came into the small airport, wondering how they worked and what it would be like to travel in them.'

I am a Yamatji man, born in Western Australia; my heritage comes from the Nhanda, Malgana and Yinggarda language groups but I have lineage up through northern Western Australia all the way to Zenadeth Kes (the Torres Strait). My traditional lands are Gutharraguda (meaning 'two bays' or 'two waters'), a place now known as Shark Bay. I was born in June 1969, one month after the death of my uncle Andrew (Andy) Drummond, who died in Vietnam while serving with the 5th Battalion, Royal Australian Regiment. I grew up in the small town of Carnarvon, in the north-west of Western Australia, about 900 kilometres north of Perth, enjoying the love and care of my mother's extended Aboriginal family. During this time, I used to marvel at the small aircraft that came into the small airport, wondering how they worked and what it would be like to travel in them.

My family then moved to Perth, where I did my secondary schooling, and, on completion of Year 12, while I applied for university, TAFE and a number of jobs, I decided to try to join the Air Force. This decision was influenced by a number of factors: firstly, I thought it would quench my love of travel (you get used to travelling long distances when you live in Western Australia); secondly, satisfy my curiosity about aircraft and air travel; thirdly, follow in the footsteps of my Uncle Andy by joining the military; and lastly, and most importantly, my father strongly suggested I join as he had fond memories being a member of the Air Training Corps in his youth.

I was successful and was recruited in Perth as a CAT2B trainee, which meant I would train to be a fitter/technician working on aircraft. The travel to RAAF Base Edinburgh in Adelaide for recruit training was from RAAF Base Pearce via a C-130 Hercules (I thought this was a great start to my career). I enjoyed my time at No 1 Recruit Training Unit, everyone was equal, treated the same and expected to 'pull their weight'. This was refreshing as I had been subjected to a fair bit of racism in my

Left: FSGT Brett West Middle East Area of Operations. (RAAF)

46

youth, although travelling into Salisbury, Elizabeth and Adelaide and being treated with disdain because of my short haircut and being a 'RAAFie', rather than the colour of my skin, was an interesting feeling.

After recruit training I was posted to RAAF Base Wagga for my aircraft fitter/technician training at the RAAF School of Technical Training. While I enjoyed the training, I started to feel homesick; I initially thought it was just missing home but soon became aware I was missing not only family, but the cultural safety of having other Aboriginal people around me (I used to joke that I would carry a mirror around with me so I could see another black RAAF face). After completing my training, I was expecting to be offered a choice of six aircraft fitter/technician roles (from working on aircraft engines and airframes through to the electronic systems) but was surprised to learn I could be an Armament Fitter (working on aircraft weapons systems, explosives and small arms weaponry) or an Aircraft Structural Fitter (working on aircraft metal and composite skins). These choices were not ideal but, after speaking to my parents, my mother helping me with feeling strong within my culture and my father giving me the confidence to see where staying in would take me, I ended up training as an Armament Fitter.

Above: Classic Hornet (RAAF)

My first posting was to RAAF Base Williamtown (WLM) in Newcastle, No 77 Squadron, on Mirages and then F/A-18 Hornets. This posting was great as the squadron travelled a lot on exercises which really satisfied my urge to travel. During this posting, the Commanding Officer asked if I would be willing to represent the squadron at Leonard Waters's funeral, the first Aboriginal fighter pilot. I accepted and found this was not only an honour but started me thinking about how successful Aboriginal people provided important role modelling for Aboriginal youth. While still at RAAF WLM, I was posted to No 2 Operational Conversion Unit, a squadron that trained pilots to fly F/A-18s, and then No 402 Wing Field Training Flight which was an Air Force technical school that trained technicians to work on F/A-18s. I enjoyed teaching and developing courses, so much so I went to university and completed an education degree. During my time at WLM, I progressed through the ranks of corporal and sergeant. I also had the opportunity to do a course known as the Aboriginal Cultural Facilitators Course which was conducted on the Anangu Pitjantjatjara Yankunytjatjara lands. This course was designed to train military personnel to be cultural facilitators for their units by providing an immersive experience in remote Aboriginal communities. I found this experience somewhat strange as the instruction was all about trying to understand the barriers and issues faced by Aboriginal society, facts I was already aware of through life experience! Oh well, it was fun being out bush and I met some good people.

My next posting (as a flight sergeant) was to Defence Establishment Orchard Hills (DEOH) to a unit called Precision Guided Munitions – Technical Maintenance Facility, which specialised in maintenance on guided missiles. This was the first time I worked in a unit that was managed by civilians (public servants) and found myself again being discriminated against for being a RAAFie (or military member) rather than my skin colour!

I then went to No 79 Squadron at RAAF Base Pearce, back to my home state and, again, involved in pilot training. As the posting was back in Perth, I was close to family and was able to go back to my Country for what I would describe as a cultural reinvigoration; while at first this was great, I found being back also involved me having cultural obligations I had not been exposed to before. Balancing these expectations along with the expectations of the Air Force was very tricky and I found the hierarchy of the squadron did not understand I had to 'walk in two worlds' that did not always converge smoothly. I never thought returning 'home' would provide me with such challenges and that the Air Force, an organisation I thought had come a long way with regards to Aboriginal inclusion, was, in fact, still fairly ignorant.

It was then back to Adelaide, to No 10 Squadron, working on the Orion maritime aircraft and for the first time I was operationally deployed, firstly as part of Operation *Resolute* (now Border Force) and then as part of the International Coalition Against Terrorism in the Middle East Area of Operations. I found the deployments good as I was able to put the training I had been doing for so many years into practice. Interestingly,

I again came across discrimination; this time, however, it was because of my mustering (trade) as Armament Fitters/Technicians were not often posted to maritime units and were 'looked down upon'.

Then came a posting back to DEOH to the newly formed Defence Explosive Ordnance Training School as the School Warrant Officer (WOFF). This school combined the training on explosives for personnel from all three Services as well as for Defence Public Servants. After this, and still at DEOH, I went to Joint Logistics Unit – Regional Explosive Ordnance Services where I performed domestic Explosive Ordnance Disposal duties (think police bomb squad) and inspections of explosive storage areas. While at these postings, I started to think about my experience at Len Waters's funeral and thought I may be able to be a role model for young Aboriginal people thinking of joining the military. To enable this, I participated in a number of Defence Indigenous Youth Programs and thoroughly enjoyed each and every course, not only seeing the development and growth of the Aboriginal participants, but also the non-Aboriginal staff who assisted. My wife then wanted to return to her home state of Victoria, so I discharged to enable our move.

For the next number of months, I was employed as a reserve and staff member for the next Indigenous Pre-Recruit Programs until being asked to come back full time into the Air Force, this time to Canberra as the WOFF for the Aboriginal and Torres Strait Islander Programs – Air Force Unit, within the Directorate of Personnel – Air Force. I was tasked with looking at Aboriginal inclusion within the Air Force and was the manager for a project looking at what the Aboriginal community wanted/needed from the Air Force. Initially, this posting was great, but I soon found that, while senior leadership understood the idea of inclusion, the management level below them was either not ready or willing to make the changes needed to make Air Force a truly culturally safe employer. I did, however, have an incredible experience travelling with the Air Force balloon unit through the central west of New South Wales, interacting with lots of Aboriginal community members, and the trip culminated in a visit to Len Waters's grave. This brought back a lot of memories and a kind of re-focus on what I wanted to achieve for the Aboriginal community which in turn led me to leave the Air Force for a second (and final) time.

Over the three decades I served, I found the Air Force to become more culturally aware and inclusive but there is still a way to go. When I first joined in the mid-80s, I faced blatant and overt racism, moving into the 90s and experiencing occasions of 'casual' racism, and going into the 21st century Air Force grappling with wanting to 'do the right thing', but not ready to make the big decisions needed to make the organisation a fully inclusive environment.

I also reflect on my time and discussions with Aboriginal colleagues about having to 'walk in two worlds', embracing our Aboriginal culture as well as the white, mainstream society and think that it's even more complex than that. Aboriginal service personnel actually have to navigate three worlds as the military culture is its own beast that sometimes collides with the other two 'worlds', providing issues that are not easily understood by non-Indigenous people.

Overall, I enjoyed my service career and still believe it is a good job to experience (I did, after all, provide stewardship for my son, nephew and niece to join) and believe there is the goodwill within the Services to bring about an even more culturally inclusive workplace.

'Over the three decades I served, I found the Air Force to become more culturally aware and inclusive but believe there is still a way to go.'

Above: Warrant Officer Brett West. (RAAF)

DAVID WILLIAM MALPAS COPLEY

Service Number: 116420
Date of Birth: 8 October 1924
Place of Birth: Plympton, South Australia
Date of Enlistment: 28 October 1942
Place of Enlistment: Adelaide, South Australia
Date of Discharge: 7 January 1946
Rank: Leading Aircraftman
Campaign: Second World War

David Copley, a Peramangk man, was born in 1924. Within days of turning 18, David applied to join the RAAF at No 5 Recruiting Centre, Adelaide. He enlisted in the RAAF for the duration of the Second World War plus 12 months. Although his previous civilian employment was that of advertising assistant, he was enlisted as a Trainee Technical with the rank of aircraftman 1.

After initial recruit training at No 1 Recruit Depot in Shepparton, Victoria, David was posted to No 1 School of Technical Training, which was located in the Exhibition Building in Carlton at the time. After successfully completing No 137 Fitters Course, in February 1943 he commenced No 43 Armourers Course at the Armament School in Hamilton, Victoria. It was a tough six-week course that commenced with 28 pupils. David was one of five who did not pass. However, after further training and passing a trade test at No 1 Engineering School (a forerunner of the current RAAF School of Technical Training) at Ascot Vale, Victoria, he remustered to Armourer and commenced work at No 2 Operational Training Unit in Mildura.

Subsequently, David returned to No 1 Recruit Depot to take part in No 10 Respirator Maintenance Course, run in June 1943 in Shepparton. Easily passing, David earned

Opposite inset: Formal RAAF photo of David Copley. (RAAF)

Opposite: An RAAF Armourer loading ammunition into one of the 20mm Hispano cannons on a Supermarine Spitfire Mk.VIII (Mitchell Library, State Library of New South Wales)

a posting to No 2 Bombing and Gunnery School at Port Pirie, South Australia. The school had been established in June 1941 to train pilots, observers and air gunners under the Empire Air Training Scheme. While at Port Pirie, David reclassified to leading aircraftman. The school disbanded on 9 December 1943 when it changed over to No 3 Air Observers School.

On the disbandment of No 2 Bombing and Gunnery School, David was posted to No 548 Squadron (Royal Air Force) which had formed at Lawnton, Queensland, before moving to Strathpine, also in Queensland, in January 1944. The squadron was manned by RAF aircrew and RAAF ground staff. Tasked with defending northern Australia against Japanese raids, the unit was equipped with the Supermarine Spitfire Mk.VIII in April 1944. Spitfires were considered more effective against Japanese raiders than the Kittyhawks then in service. Pending the arrival of the Spitfires, the squadron trained with Wirraway and Tiger Moth aircraft at Lawnton and Petrie Airfields in Queensland. After re-equipping, the squadron then made several moves: to RAAF Amberley, Queensland; to Livingstone Airfield, Northern Territory; and then to Darwin on 22 October 1944. The squadron also maintained a detachment at Truscott Airfield on the Anjo Peninsula in Western Australia.

While in Darwin, No 548 Squadron's primary role was to intercept incoming Japanese raiders. By the time hostilities in the Pacific ended in August 1945, the squadron had only completed two offensive missions, a sweep over Selaroe Island and an attack on the Japanese airfield at Cape Chater, Timor. The squadron proceeded to No 1 Personnel Depot in Melbourne in September 1945 and disbanded on 31 October.

David posted out of the squadron to the RAAF's No 2 Squadron with effect from 24 January 1945. During this time, the squadron was involved in anti-shipping operations. During March and April, the unit moved progressively to Jacquinot Bay in New Britain while continuing operations from Hughes, near Darwin. It was a welcome move that had been long awaited as the Allies had captured the area from the Japanese in late 1944. However, David remained in Australia and, for a short period from late May, was attached for duty with No 7 Repair and Salvage Unit in Darwin. In that month, the unit's Armament Section was conducting inspections on Spitfires and Mitchells in addition to their regular maintenance, servicing and modification work.

On 12 June, David embarked for Balikpapan, Borneo, where, after operating for nearly seven months with equipment and personnel scattered about the theatre, No 2 Squadron eventually settled. With hostilities in the Pacific ending on 15 August, personnel commenced returning to Australia and eventual demobilisation. David began his journey home on 11 September 1945, disembarking on 5 October, and reported to No 4 Personnel Depot at Springbank, South Australia. He was then briefly posted to No 6 Service Flying Training School at RAAF Mallala, South Australia, on 26 November before returning to No 4 Personnel Depot for his discharge.

Leading Aircraftman David Copley completed his discharge on 7 January 1946.

Above: North American B-25D Mitchells A47-16/KO-L and A47-7/KO-S of No 2 Squadron at Hughes Field, Northern Territory. (RAAF)

Opposite: Armourers fitting belts of ammunition to the machine guns in the nose of a Wirraway. (State Library Victoria, Argus Collection)

AILEEN ROSE DANIELSON (NEE BELL)

Service Number: W125327
Date of Birth: 30 July 1958
Place of Birth: Brisbane, Queensland
Date of Enlistment: 11 April 1977
Place of Enlistment: Brisbane, Queensland
Date of Discharge: 24 May 1985
Rank: Corporal

My Defence family has always been there for me and I know they will always be my family.

I am an Aboriginal woman who grew up in Inala, Brisbane. I was fortunate having a good family, opportunities and, with a lot of hard work, I was able to finish my Junior High School Certificate at Richlands State High. I then completed a year of Business School (Office Skills) at Kangaroo Point Technical College. From here I was able to gain a full-time position with Telstra (then called Telecom Australia) in Fortitude Valley, Brisbane. It was at this time that I felt my life was very mundane. I came across an uncle who was a serving member of the Navy and then the Air Force; his name is Phillip Bell. Having spent some time with him, and seeing how much he knew, the travelling he was able to do, and how the Air Force really looked after him and his family, I knew then this was a career where I could achieve and grow. It was my best light bulb moment ever. It gave me the confidence to be able to leave home knowing I would be looked after.

The old recruitment centre in Brisbane was absolutely fantastic, the encouragement and support they gave was amazing for such a young girl. It would take me over two hours – by bus, train, and walking – each time I had to go into the centre.

Formal photo of Aileen Bell. (RAAF)

ALL SMILES, after signing up for the Royal Australian Air Force, are these local lasses.

Pictured is WRAAF Corporal, Roslyn Cameron (left), showing new recruits, Pamela Duran, 20, of Camp Hill, Doris Beattie, 21, of Sherwood, Audrey Pope, 16, of Murarrie, and Aileen Bell, 18, of Inala, something of what

Walking on air!

to expect in the WRAAF.

The girls are pictured at the Joint Services Recruiting Centre, Brisbane.

But, by now, they'll be installed in the Air Force's Victorian basic training centre, at Laverton.

The girls will undergo a five-week training course

and will be able to choose from a variety of careers offered by the Air Force.

Pam and Doris have already set their sights on becoming medical orderlies.

Murarrie girl, Audrey, would like to work on the RAAF switchboard.

Aileen has an initial desire to become a supply clerk — an important administrative job ensuring bases all over Australia are kept up to date.

But one thing's for sure girls' careers take them, they're in the Air Force now!

Above: Photo from a newspaper article on Aileen joining the WRAAF. (Aileen Danielson)

Opposite: Women's Royal Australian Air Force course photo, group 246B. Aileen is in 2nd row, 1st from Right. (RAAF)

When I enlisted, we had a very large Women's Royal Australian Air Force (WRAAF) intake of approximately 100 women, so the course was split into two groups, 246A and 246B (my group). My course was at Radschool (the School of Radio), Block 100, Laverton, in Victoria. We were the very last WRAAF course ever. The men always teased us and barked, because we were WRAAFs (Woofs), and believed we would be gone within six months once we found a husband.

After my recruit course, I commenced training in Wagga Wagga. As it was such a large intake, they were short of female accommodation, so we were quickly accommodated into an old, cold, suddenly empty, Apprentice Block in the middle of winter. There was no privacy and constant toilet flushing, day and night. After training, I was posted to RAAF Base Richmond; firstly to 2AD (Aircraft Depot) Richmond, Base Squadron Richmond, and then to No 37 Squadron.

Living on base at Richmond was great; I had my own single room. This was the first time in my life I had my own room. There were not a lot of women living on base, but we did get to eat in a special annex room off the Sergeants Mess as this was a lot closer for us than walking the distance to the Airmens Mess. The food was fantastic; we could order our eggs cooked anyway we wanted! No complaints at all. We were treated pretty special when it came to food.

I remember one time when I was in hospital at Richmond, No 3 RAAF, in the women's ward, all by myself. We had our usual morning Matron inspection and, would you believe, every morning I had to have my bed made and I had to stand at attention beside my bed while she walked through. All while being sick …

I married on 12 April 1981, while still serving, to an ex-RAAF man, Barry Colin Danielson. After my marriage, I applied for a married quarter. They discovered I had married a non-serving member and was therefore not entitled to a married quarter. The paperwork took months and months; just to fight for equality for housing and accommodation was a nightmare. After my posting to 2AD, I struck it lucky and was posted to Base Squadron Barracks, the exact unit that looked after and handled all the married quarters.

Following this, I was posted to No 37 Squadron, they were flying Hercules, and was the first female (corporal) ever posted there. While at the squadron, there were no female toilets or facilities available; I had to walk some distance to find suitable toilets. I clearly remember carrying a bell around with me and I would ring this before entering flight crew areas just in case they were undressed or swearing. I loved every minute of it.

I have only recently found out that at least one of my great-great-uncles served as a Light Horse man in the First World War and survived. Pretty good for an Aboriginal man, although I believe life after the war at home was pretty hard. One was buried in a pauper's grave, but that has recently been redone by the Department of Defence, some 100 years later.

Joining the Air Force in 1977 was the best thing I had ever done. My Defence family has always been there for me and I know they will always be my family.

> *I clearly remember carrying a bell around with me and I would ring this before entering flight crew areas just in case they were undressed or swearing.*

TRAMAINE DUKES

Date of Birth: 7 May 1984
Place of Birth: Tom Price, Western Australia
Date of Enlistment: 14 October 2019
Place of Enlistment: Perth, Western Australia
Rank: Flight Lieutenant

> *Hearing the Chief of Air Force, Air Marshal Mel Hupfeld, speak in Ngunnawal language for his entire speech hit the heart strings for all of us.*

My mob is the Mara mob from the Northern Territory. We are predominantly saltwater people located on the east coast of the NT, part of the Gulf of Carpentaria, but we also have access to the freshwater Roper River. I grew up on Whadjuk Noongar Boodja (Perth metro area, Western Australia).

I joined the Royal Australian Air Force in October 2019 as an Indigenous Liaison Officer (ILO). I was part of the 'Recruit When Ready' program and started at RAAF Base Pearce in Perth before attending Officer Training School on 20 January 2020. I come from a family of service personnel; my father, Leading Aircraftman Brett David Dukes, served for six years as a Telecommunications Technician and my mother, Leading Aircraftwoman Karen Lucie Oppermann (Dukes), served in the Air Force for three years as a Communications Operator. So, I was destined to join as well.

My officer training was ever flexible, with the first six weeks conducted at RAAF Base Wagga due to Operation *Bushfire Assist* being run out of RAAF Base East Sale. Then shortly after being able to return to East Sale to continue our training there, the COVID-19 pandemic struck, turning our entire training upside down. We were the first Initial Officer Course in history to graduate during a global pandemic on 14 May 2020.

Flight Lieutenant Tramaine Dukes outside RAAF Base Pearce during NAIDOC Week 2020. (RAAF)

On completion of my officer training, I returned to my new role as an Indigenous Liaison Officer at RAAF Base Pearce. My time here has been extremely rewarding and within a short space of time I organised the first ever Welcome to Country and Smoking Ceremony for No 2 Flying Training School's (2FTS) graduation parade. These are now standard ceremonies and integral parts of all future 2FTS graduation parades. I have been a guest speaker at the Banksia Juvenile Detention Centre for the young women graduating in the Australian Army Cadet program. I have had the honour of being acknowledged on centre court by the Perth Wildcats basketball team, during their opening home game in January 2021, as an Indigenous Service person. I have also supported the Indigenous Youth Program in Townsville. We spent three full days with 11 young Aboriginal women and men, showcasing what a life in the Air Force can offer them. At the end of these three days, it was fantastic to see all 11 students complete an application to join the ADF. This was one of the most rewarding times of my short career in the Air Force. I 100 per cent believe that, at the end of this program, these amazing humans taught me a lot more than what I taught them.

" *I wish I had joined earlier.* "

Above: The Royal Australian Air Force Centenary opening ceremony. (RAAF)
Opposite: Trevor Walley, Whadjuk Noongar Elder, with Flight Lieutenant Tramaine Dukes, during No 25 Squadron's Freedom of Entry parade in the City of Perth, Western Australia. (RAAF)

As an Indigenous Liaison Officer, my role is to enhance Air Force's capability through increased engagement with the Indigenous community both externally and internally. I build relationships between the Aboriginal community and RAAF Bases Pearce and Learmonth personnel. For the most part, I want to work myself out of a job! I aim for everything that I do to become 'business as usual' so the RAAF (or ultimately the ADF) doesn't need a specific mustering for Aboriginal culture and that everyone just knows to incorporate and acknowledge Aboriginal culture in everything we do.

My proudest and most memorable moment to date was during the opening commemorations for the Air Force's 100th birthday in 2021. As the ILO mustering is very new to the RAAF, all of the ILOs were invited to attend all of the events during the opening week. This showed me just how highly regarded Aboriginal and Torres Strait Islander culture is by the RAAF and the Chief of Air Force. What we, as ILOs, are doing for Australia's First Nations Peoples isn't just tokenistic; we are (along with the Air Force) paving the way for future generations to come. The entire 'Soil Collection' event – where shells, soil and sand collected from around Australia were enshrined at the Australian War Memorial as part of the 'For Our Country' – Aboriginal and Torres Strait Islander memorial – was one of the most humbling experiences in my life and hearing the Chief of Air Force, Air Marshal Mel Hupfeld, speak in Ngunnawal language for his entire speech hit the heart strings for all of us.

I think the best quote summing up my time in the Air Force so far is: 'Per ardua ad astra – through adversity to the stars'. I strive for a better future, reaching for the stars, and beyond, not only for myself, but for my family, my mob and my people.

MICHAEL JOHN ELLIS

Service Number: A43677
Date of Birth: 26 October 1940
Place of Birth: Darwin, Northern Territory
Date of Enlistment: 4 April 1961
Place of Enlistment: Adelaide, South Australia
Date of Discharge: 1 June 1981
Rank: Sergeant
Conflict: Vietnam War

Above: RAAF DHC-4 Caribou A4-208. (RAAF)
Opposite: Airframe Fitter Leading Aircraftman Kevin Martin and Aircraft Metal Worker Leading Aircraftman
Michael Ellis work on a wing section of a Caribou inside a hangar at Vung Tau. (Australian War Memorial)

Michael was born in Darwin in 1940. Aged 21 and living in South Australia, he enlisted
in the RAAF as an Aircraft Metal Worker with the rank of aircraftman. On his enlistment
application he cited he wanted to join the RAAF for job security and to gain experience
in aircraft metal trades. He had already completed a trade certificate as a metal worker
and, on 14 March 1961, completed a five-year apprenticeship with Clarkson Ltd in
South Australia. Although his enlistment was for an initial period of six years, Michael
extended his service to just beyond 20 years by re-engaging for specified periods on
multiple occasions.

Michael's Air Force career began at No 1 Recruit Training Unit at RAAF Base Wagga,
New South Wales, where he joined 34 other recruits in completing the ten-week-long
No 561 Recruit Training Course which ended on 23 June 1961. After recruit training,
Michael was first posted to No 1 Basic Flying Training School (1BFTS) at RAAF Point
Cook, Victoria. The school had been formed ten years earlier at Uranquinty, New South
Wales, before moving to Point Cook in December 1958. It was subsequently renamed
No 1 Flying Training School and is now based at RAAF East Sale, Victoria. In 1961,
the school was equipped with Winjeel trainers in which RAAF Academy cadet pilots
received their initial flying training. Tragically, just as Michael was posted in, a cadet and

instructor were killed when one of these aircraft crashed. On 5 July 1962, while still at 1BFTS, he reclassified to leading aircraftman after successfully completing the required examinations. While not technically a promotion, reclassification came with higher pay and additional responsibilities, and also positioned him for promotion.

At the beginning of 1964, Michael was posted to No 2 Aircraft Depot at RAAF Base Richmond. At the time, No 10 Squadron, operating Neptunes, and No 86 Wing's transport squadrons, flying C-47 Dakotas and C-130A Hercules, were based at Richmond. The depot provided deeper maintenance for these types. For Michael, it represented a significant step up from carrying out metal work on Winjeels. He remained at the depot for two years where his superiors remarked on his efficiency, dependability and keenness to learn. While there, Michael also undertook further studies at a technical school in his own time. These attributes led to him being selected for service in Vietnam. Such postings were highly sought after and highly competitive.

Posted to the RAAF Transport Flight Vietnam, Michael arrived at Vung Tau, South Vietnam, in September 1965. Locally known as 'Wallaby Airlines' due to its callsign *Wallaby,* the flight had formed at RAAF Butterworth, Malaysia, on 20 July 1964 and was the first RAAF unit to deploy to the Vietnam War. Prior to being renamed No 35 Squadron in June 1966, the flight completed 16,853 sorties, transporting 78,662 passengers and delivering 12,950 tonnes of freight and 118 tonnes of mail between Vung Tau, Tan Son Nhat and Pleiku. Michael carried out metal work repairs to the flight's DHC-4 Caribou aircraft damaged by Viet Cong gun and mortar fire. As he departed on posting to No 2 Aircraft Depot in Australia in mid-1966, Michael was described as a willing, energetic worker in a particularly hard-working section who was 'fit now' for promotion. He was duly promoted to corporal on 1 April 1967. Members of the RAAF Transport Flight Vietnam, and those of No 35 Squadron, who served in Vietnam from August 1964 to February 1972 have earned the right to wear the Republic of Vietnam Cross of Gallantry.

Michael remained at No 2 Aircraft Depot between 1967 and 1973 where he resumed work on Neptune and Hercules aircraft, including the new C-130E variant of the famous transport. He also worked on the new P-3B Orions as well as UH-1H Iroquois and Caribous. In 1970, Michael experienced the disappointment of a cancelled overseas posting. His spirits and performance lifted again when another overseas posting was in the offing, this time to No 478 (Maintenance) Squadron at RAAF Butterworth. Michael was at Butterworth from 10 July 1973 to 16 July 1976. On this occasion, he was accompanied by his family. The squadron provided maintenance support to the Mirages of No 75 Squadron that formed part of Australia's contribution to the ongoing Five Power Defence Arrangements, established in 1971, between the United Kingdom, Australia, New Zealand, Malaysia and Singapore. Initially, RAAF fighter squadrons had deployed to Butterworth in late 1958–early 1959 in response to the Malayan Emergency and had remained during the confrontation with Indonesia in the 1960s. After the

No 478 (Maintenance) Squadron at RAAF Butterworth. The squadron provided maintenance support to the Mirages. (RAAF)

United Kingdom withdrew its forces from east of the Suez Canal in the early 1970s, RAAF fighter units were deployed to Butterworth until 1988.

Throughout his time with No 478 Squadron, Michael's technical skills and acceptance of responsibility were remarked upon. Having undertaken the necessary training and examinations, he was again well-positioned for promotion. Michael was promoted to sergeant on 1 November 1973. Even though he was newly promoted, he was earning superior assessments at No 478 Squadron. In addition, Michael was quite ambitious in developing his trade and supervisory skills. He completed many internal courses including Iroquois Technical Conversion, Non-destructive Inspection Supervisor, Mirage Boron Fibre Repairs and Sergeant Supervision and Management.

After Butterworth, Michael was posted, with effect from 16 July 1976, to No 481 Squadron at RAAF Williamtown and was placed in charge of the Aircraft Metal Work Section of the Aircraft Maintenance Flight. Moreover, he was the only senior non-commissioned officer aircraft metal worker on the base supervising metal work on the ageing Macchi, Mirage, Winjeel and Iroquois fleets; this entailed complicated metal repairs and a high workload. Shortly after Michael's arrival, the Commanding Officer reported increasing workloads across the squadron due to high flying rates and the loss of expertise due to a major changeover of staff. Michael's workload increased as he was called on to control and supervise additional personnel. Michael continued at No 481 Squadron until he discharged from the Air Force after 20 years' service.

Sergeant Michael Ellis left the RAAF on 1 June 1981.

GEORGE TONGERIE

Service Number: 140638
Date of Birth: 28 February 1925
Place of Birth: Quorn, South Australia
Date of Enlistment: 29 June 1943
Place of Enlistment: Adelaide, South Australia
Date of Discharge: 14 February 1946
Rank: Leading Aircraftman
Campaign: Second World War

Above: Colebrook Children's Home in Quorn, South Australia. (George Tongerie)

Opposite: Portrait image of George Tongerie that is now centrepiece of a display at RAAF Edinburgh's Airmen's Club. The image was provide by Uncle George's family. (Air Force Association – South Australian Division)

George Tongerie was born in 1925 in Quorn, a town in South Australia's Flinders Ranges. At the age of 18 he enlisted at No 5 Recruit Centre in Adelaide in the General Hand mustering with the rank of aircraftman 1. On his enlistment application, George recorded his civilian occupation as tanner's assistant.

Immediately after enlistment, George completed No 1032 Recruit Drill Course at No 1 Recruit Depot at Shepparton, Victoria, after which he was posted to Headquarters RAAF Laverton, also in Victoria. On 30 September 1943, he was posted to No 2 Embarkation Depot at Bradfield Park, New South Wales. This was followed in October by postings to No 1 Reserve Personnel Pool at Aitkenvale and to No 8 Stores Depot at Townsville, both in Queensland. During the latter posting, George reclassified to leading aircraftman.

On 18 April 1944, George arrived at No 12 Squadron at Merauke in what, at the time, was Netherlands New Guinea (now a province of Indonesia). The squadron had formed at Laverton on 6 February 1939 but delayed its planned move to Darwin until July due to a shortage of aircraft. Stationed at the Temporary Hutted Camp at Darwin's civilian aerodrome, and equipped with Avro Ansons and Wirraways, No 12 Squadron was the first RAAF unit to be permanently based at Darwin. From there, it conducted maritime and anti-submarine patrols in defence of northern Australia. In late 1942, the squadron re-equipped with Vultee Vengeance dive bombers, operating from various airfields in the Northern Territory and conducting maritime and anti-submarine patrols until it moved to Merauke in November 1943. In mid-1944, No 12 Squadron moved to Queensland where it re-equipped with B-24 Liberator heavy bombers. It disbanded in 1948, re-forming as No 1 Squadron.

When the squadron moved to Queensland in mid-1944 to convert to Liberators, George remained at Merauke and, on 11 July, moved 'next door' to No 44 Operational Base Unit which had arrived a year earlier. The unit controlled personnel who provided airfield support services, including fire fighters, medical orderlies, the duty crew and air traffic controllers. By 1944, as combat operations had moved further north and west, the unit provided a staging camp (accommodation and messing facilities) for personnel moving through the area.

George returned to Australia, having spent nearly 15 months in a forward area of operations. He arrived at No 4 Personnel Depot at Springbank, South Australia, in July 1945. He then had consecutive postings in New South Wales, at No 17 Replenishing Centre in Bowral and Headquarters No 5 (Maintenance) Group in Sydney, before reporting back to No 4 Personnel Depot for discharge.

Leading Aircraftman George Tongerie discharged from the RAAF on 14 February 1946.

From the Stolen Generation to serving his country during the Second World War, Leading Aircraftman George Tongerie was an advocate for Aboriginal and Torres Strait Islander rights and education. Despite having served his country with pride, after he discharged he encountered the same racial issues he knew before the war. That led him and his wife to become active members of the Aboriginal Progress Association during the 1960s and he became a role model for Aboriginal and Torres Strait Islander activism for many years. He was also vice-president of the National Aboriginal and Torres Strait Islander Veterans Association and marched regularly on Anzac Day.

George was instrumental in championing the efforts to create Australia's first memorial to Aboriginal servicemen and women in Adelaide. A committee was established to raise the funds required to build the memorial and it took just four months to raise the $740,000 needed for the memorial to be built, at the foot of the Torrens Parade Ground on King William Road. At the time the memorial was built, George was the oldest First Nations ex-serviceman in South Australia. Knowing the dream had become a reality put a smile on his face.

Private Robert Angove (left) and Flight Sergeant Gary Browning (right) with South Australia's oldest surviving Aboriginal serviceman, George Tongarie, at Highgate. (Simon Cross, *The Advertiser*)

COEN HENRY

Date of Birth: 7 August 1988
Place of Birth: Blacktown, New South Wales
Date of Enlistment: 26 April 2011
Place of Enlistment: New South Wales
Rank: Flying Officer

> *If you want to go fast, go alone. If you want to go far, go together.*

I was born in Blacktown Hospital in 1988 and raised in a housing commission house in a small suburb named Willmot in the back of Mount Druitt. I was raised in Dharug nation, which expands from Parramatta to the mountains. Despite my upbringing, my bloodlines connect to the Paakantji/Maraura and Wiradjuri tribes through my grandmother and grandfather on my father's side.

Above: Custom artwork presented in 2021. (Coen Henry)
Bottom left: Solo NAIDOC Week Performance/Art Presentation (2014 – Op *Slipper*/Op *Accordion*). (Coen Henry)
Bottom right: Senior Indigenous Liaison Officer – Custom artwork presented to WGCDR Cheryl Neal. (Coen Henry)
Opposite: Initial Officers Course 05/21 – Officer Training School, RAAF Base East Sale. (Coen Henry)

 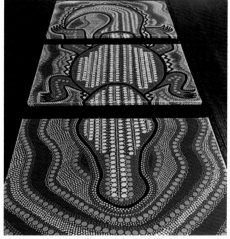

Left: Solo NAIDOC Week Performance/Art Presentation (2014 – Op *Slipper*/Op *Accordion*). (Coen Henry)
Right: Most recent piece entered in the *2022 Napier Waller Art Prize* at the Australian War Memorial. (Coen Henry)

Throughout my adolescence, the most important stories were art and dance. Aboriginal and Torres Strait Islanders tell their stories through various means and the significance varies based on the occasion and audience. Aunty Sandra Hickey was our Aboriginal Support Officer growing up and a part of the school network, which performed all around Sydney for various events to showcase our culture and means of reconciliation.

My interest in joining the Air Force started with Warrant Officer Col Watego in a chance encounter at the Mount Druitt Shopping Centre in 2007. As we now refer to him, Uncle Col challenged my mates and me about whether we were brave enough to join. My friends saw him as a government figure of power and influence. I saw him as a proud First Nations man trying to help his people. Fast-forward 14 years after completing a decade of service, the answer is "Yes, I am, Uncle, yes, I am."

Senior Elder Uncle Wes Marne (almost one hundred) told me when I was young, 'Our culture is about common sense and taking only what you need from Mother Nature, and survival, our people have been doing this for sixty thousand years.' The cultural significance I find in my service is to serve to protect our land, waterways and airways, and my culture and mob, and to support my family and community so they don't have to bear arms and potentially be put in harm's way. For the love of my ancestors, people, loved ones, and the next generation's motivation to wear the blue cams with pride.

My life before Air Force hung in the balance by constantly avoiding crime, drugs, gangs and incarceration. It was an ongoing battle to secure full-time employment due to employers' perceptions of where I was from and where I reside. If it wasn't for the Air

Force, there is a strong chance I would be dead or incarcerated; unfortunately, most of my friends growing up have gone down this path, which inspires me to be my best and be a positive role model to my family and community.

The Air Force has satisfied my expectations for the most part as an employer of choice. There has been plenty of opportunities and support along the way. In addition, like most large organisations, there is room for improvement, especially in the cultural space. Many people in Indigenous Affairs have done and continue to provide significant in-roads for the First Nation servicemen and women. However, there is still more to be done to close the gap and support recruitment and retention initiatives. It is the driving factor behind deciding to become an Indigenous Liaison Officer, instead of a Logistics Officer, as my passion for my mob runs deep.

I have undertaken a lot of training courses and my experiences throughout were quite rewarding; there were challenges given my circumstances, although the pursuit of excellence through professional development got me through. This pathway enabled me to accomplish my goal of becoming an Indigenous Liaison Officer and be in a privileged position to give back to the organisation and community.

The small circle of mates I have in the Air Force are a select group of people I trust wholeheartedly with my life. The bond we have, and the shared experiences, is invaluable and will never be taken for granted. I thought I knew what mateship was until I joined Air Force, then my perspective changed.

When I return home to my mob and tribe, I am always met with positivity and my mob and Elders make the extra effort to have a modern-day corroboree. Taking the skills I have learned through my training with the Air Force and sharing them with my community enhances the cross-cultural immersion experience. The only downside is there is never enough time, as the family want more, as I often don't get enough due to capability requirements.

Currently, I am posted to No 22 Squadron as the Indigenous Liaison Officer at RAAF Base Richmond in charge of the Greater Sydney Region and the link between the four Traditional Custodian tribes, consisting of Dharug, Gundungarra, Eora and Tharawal, and the Air Force Bases/Establishments, where we raise, train and sustain, including RAAF Base Richmond, Glenbrook and Defence Establishment Orchard Hills. My role and responsibilities focus on cultural awareness, cultural guidance, retention, recruitment and community engagement.

It's through my work here that I am inspired to support the whole of government efforts to 'Close the Gap' and reach 5 per cent recruitment and retention across the Air Force, Army, Navy and Australian Public Service. There is a need for further education and a shift from a fourth-generation mindset to a fifth-generation one, which is more inclusive and open to diversity in our workplace, procedures, customs and traditions. Nonetheless, miracles don't happen overnight, and Rome wasn't built in a day. I am optimistic we will reconcile and bridge these gaps with exemplary leadership and influence.

Becoming an Indigenous Liaison Officer in 2021 is the culmination of a decade of planning, recruit training, postings, exercises, deployments, promotions, and Initial Officers Course; I am finally here and never lost sight.

The privilege and honour to represent my people, culture and community contributed to selecting the Indigenous Liaison Officer role over the Logistics Officer (LOGO) specialisation to commence my career as a junior officer. The intent is to specialise as a LOGO upon accomplishing my goals in the cultural space.

I hope more Air Force personnel understand the meaning of 'Defending Country' before I depart the organisation. For me, it is about protecting my bloodline, songlines, ancestors' legacy, my culture, the land, waterways and airways, the emerging leaders of the next generation, our nation's values, diversity, and way of life. My Elders and ancestors have been defending these lands for tens of thousands of years. It is an honour I carry with great pride to support the Air Force and Greater Sydney region and enhance partnerships and opportunities in alignment with the Defence Reconciliation Action Plan and Air Force Indigenous Engagement strategies.

Senior Elder Uncle Wes Marne mentioned a quote to me, and it echoes, 'If you want to go fast, go alone. If you want to go far, go together.' Culture is about three things, common sense, only taking what you need and survival.

> *Our culture is about common sense and taking only what you need from Mother Nature, and survival, our people have been doing this for sixty thousand years.*

Opposite: Major General Craig Orme (Rtd.) and then Leading Aircraftman Coen Henry. (Coen Henry)

KRISTAL HOUSE

Date of Birth: 7 January 1986
Place of Birth: Ipswich, Queensland
Date of Enlistment: 10 August 2018
Rank: Flight Lieutenant

> *I have made friendships since being in*
> *Air Force that will last for a lifetime.*

I was born in Ipswich, Queensland, on 7 January 1986. My mother's country is Bidjara and my father's is Nunukul.

My family has a strong service history with several of my family serving in the Army going back to the First World War; they were always Army, none of my family have served in the Air Force or Navy until now. So, my family was a little horrified when I told them I was joining the Air Force instead of the Army. I had a real desire to be able to showcase Indigenous culture and serve our country, so I joined on 10 August 2018 to become an Indigenous Liaison Officer. Longer term, I would like to study to further my career in the RAAF and enhance my understanding of international relations. A goal of mine is to become an Operations Officer and work in an embassy in the South Pacific region as my great-grandmother is Melanesian from Rotuma.

In my short time with the Air Force, one of my most memorable moments has been doing Christmas drops in remote communities. Being able to deliver a little bit of hope and joy to these communities provided a real sense of achievement.

Opposite: Flight Lieutenant Kristal House talks with Deputy Chair of the Kauareg Native Title Elizah Wasaga on the King's Point beach at Ngurupai (Horn Island) in the Torres Strait. (RAAF)

Above: Air Commander Australia, Officer Commanding No 84 Wing and Commanding Officer No 35 Squadron visit Horn and Thursday Islands in northern Queensland to pay their respects to the local Torres Strait Islander community. (RAAF)

One of the most rewarding experiences I was a part of was in the lead up to the Centenary of Air Force. Aboriginal and Torres Strait Islander communities, together with Air Force personnel, gathered samples from places of significance around the country. These samples of shells, soil and sand then formed an integral part of the Welcome Ceremony for Air Force's Centenary birthday that was held in 2021. This was an acknowledgement of Air Force's footprint being on traditional land around Australia. I was sent to King's Point beach at Ngurupai (Horn Island), in the Torres Strait, where we met with members of the Kuarareg tribe, and gathered shells to symbolise the strong partnership between the Torres Strait Islander people and the Air Force. Our relationship with the community on Horn and Thursday Islands is invaluable and the local traditions are recognised with the highest respect. The ADF is proud of its Aboriginal and Torres Strait Islander men and women who have contributed to the defence of Australia in times of peace and war.

Since joining, I have been extremely proud of being a First Nations person and serving our country; it is the ultimate honour and privilege. Being a role model to younger generations is an extra special bonus to this.

" *Mateship means everything.* "

Above: Yuggera Elders, Aunty Maria Davidson and Aunty Lilly Davidson, present a commemorative box filled with soil and gum leaves to Group Captain Iain Carty as Ugarapul Elders, Uncle Ross Anderson and Aunty Roberta Graham, present their commemorative box to Indigenous Liaison Officer Flight Lieutenant Kristal House. (RAAF)

Opposite: Flight Lieutenant Kristal House with Australian Army Lance Corporal Josephane Naawi from 51st Battalion, Far North Queensland Regiment, and her grandchild, on Masig (Yorke Island) during No 35 Squadron's Exercise *Christmas Hop*, which delivered supplies to remote Aboriginal and Torres Strait Islander communities in Far North Queensland ahead of the holiday season. (RAAF)

LEONARD VICTOR WATERS

Service Number: 78144
Date of Birth: 20 June 1924
Place of Birth: Boomi, New South Wales
Date of Enlistment: 24 August 1942
Rank: Warrant Officer
Campaign: Second World War

'I grew up in the era when the skies were being explored. There was Amy Johnson, Kingsford Smith, Bert Hinkler, Lindbergh, and Jean Batten in New Zealand, and when other kids were making toys – this was when I was only about eight or nine years of age – and while the other kids were playing with ordinary toys, I'd be making model planes and flying kites. I always, as people have said, had my "head in the clouds". Unfortunately, it took a world war for me to realise my ambition, but, fortunately for me, I did do that.'

Len Waters was born in mid-1924 at Boomi in northern New South Wales. He enlisted in the RAAF on 24 August 1942; he actually tried to join a year earlier when he was only 17 but was turned away and told to come back when he was 18. Len was originally selected as ground crew (fitter) but, through perseverance and study, he was accepted for aircrew. Len was one of among the earliest men of Aboriginal heritage to be accepted for pilot training.

He did his initial flying training at No 1 Elementary Training Flying School, Narrandera, in the Riverina region of New South Wales, graduating as a sergeant pilot from No 5 Service Flying Training School, at Uranquinty, a town just south of Wagga Wagga. He continued his training at No 2 Operational Training Unit across the border in Mildura. From there he was posted to No 78 Squadron on 14 November 1944. He had his first flight with the squadron on the 17th and flew his first operational sortie on the 24th. A dive-bombing attack on an enemy airstrip, Len recorded his 'Bombs fell wide of target'. He flew his second dive-bombing sortie the next day.

Opposite: Len in his full winter flying suit at Narrandera, New South Wales, 1943. (Australian War Memorial)

I always, as people have said,
had my 'head in the clouds'.

Above: Len's P-40 Kittyhawk. (Australian War Memorial)

Opposite left: Len being presented with his wings, July 1944. (Australian War Memorial)

Opposite right: Len on Morotai, 1945, relaxing in the squadron's tent lines. (Australian War Memorial)

Opposite bottom: Len on Morotai with fellow members of No 78 Squadron. (Australian War Memorial)

In mid-January 1945, he was amused to be allocated a Kittyhawk with the name 'Black Magic' painted on its nose (by a pilot who had left the squadron tour-expired). The name appealed to Len, so he kept it. Based at Noemfoor, Dutch New Guinea, Morotai, and Tarakan, and with encounters with the Japanese in the air few and far between, the squadron was heavily involved in attacking Japanese ground forces and installations. Len saw several of his mates killed while carrying out these ground attacks; the Japanese might have been scarce in the air, but they continued to vigorously defend their positions with heavy anti-aircraft fire.

On one of these sorties, an unexploded 35mm high explosive shell lodged itself in the cockpit of the Kittyhawk, just behind his head. Realising the trouble he was in, Len flew the two and half hours back to base, landing without further incident. 'I landed on egg shells that day.'

Len completed 95 sorties – 41 strikes and 54 other operational flights – ending the war as a warrant officer.

Remembering his time in the RAAF as a fighter pilot, Len said, 'People would often ask me about discrimination, and was I ever discriminated against. Now, I can say, no, I was not ever. And, as a matter of fact, two of my best friends, they came from high-class families in Sydney, and I was always accepted as equal to them.'

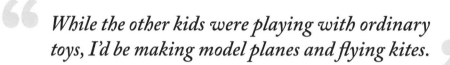

While the other kids were playing with ordinary toys, I'd be making model planes and flying kites.

Above: Len (back row, second from left) with fellow pilots at Mildura, Victoria, in 1944. (Australian War Memorial)

Opposite: Len in the cockpit of his Kittyhawk. (Australian War Memorial)

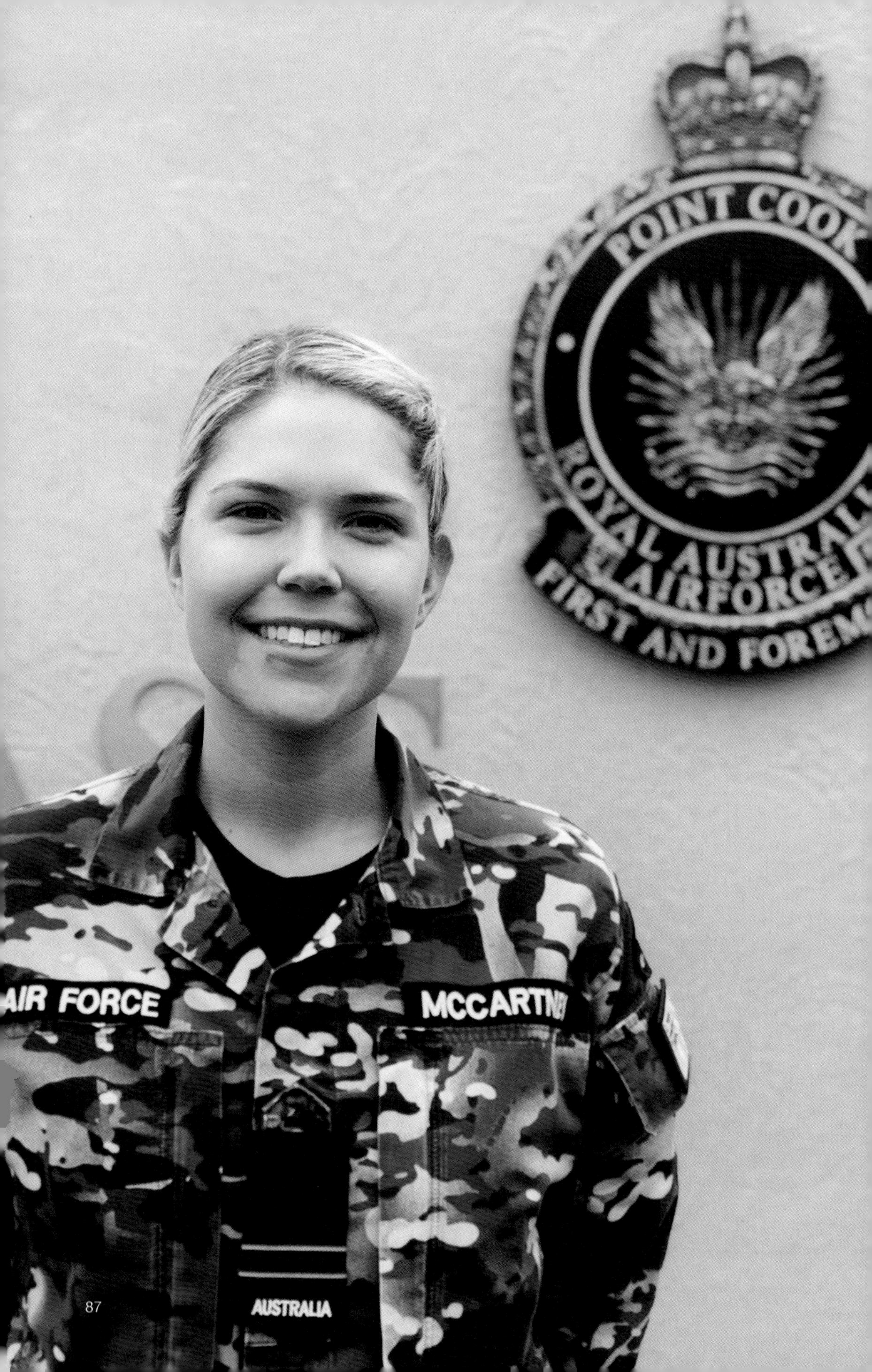
POINT COOK
AIRFORCE
AIR FORCE
AUSTRALIA

AIMEE McCARTNEY

Date of Birth: 13 July 1992
Place of Birth: Melbourne, Victoria
Date of Enlistment 10 August 2018
Place of Enlistment: Melbourne, Victoria
Rank: Flight Lieutenant

I was born in Melbourne, Victoria, away from my family's traditional lands, but I maintain my heritage as a proud Taungurung and Wotjobaluk woman; these countries are to the north of Melbourne and in the north-west of Victoria respectively.

After completing primary school at Preston South Primary School, I was offered and accepted a scholarship to attend Ivanhoe Girls Grammar near Melbourne. While I struggled a little with Maths and English, I thrived on sports. I participated in anything I could get into, including cricket, volleyball, netball, basketball, and represented my school in Little Athletics.

During my school years, I was introduced to Defence service through my experiences as a cadet with 39 Army Cadet Unit at Simpson Barracks.

I went on to complete a Bachelor of Arts, majoring in Archaeology and History and, as there were few opportunities for graduates in these areas, I joined the Victorian State Public Service until being offered a position in the Air Force as an Indigenous Liaison Officer.

Insofar as my family's military background goes, my great-great-great-grandfather, Private Alfred Jackson Coombs, served during the First World War alongside his brothers Cecil and Willy in the 59th Battalion AIF. At least 15 members of my family have served in the armed forces from the Second World War through to the modern day.

I joined the Air Force on 10 August 2018, taking up a position at RAAF Base Point Cook as the Indigenous Liaison Officer. After three years at Point Cook, I moved to RAAF Base East Sale and I am looking forward to working with the Gunaikurnai community.

Opposite: Aimee at Point Cook. (RAAF)

Above: Flight Lieutenant Aimee McCartney, Private Kirra Grimes and Leading Seaman Henry Burns perform with their traditional instruments during the new Australian National Anthem recording at Alan Eaton Studios in St Kilda, Melbourne, Victoria. (RAAF)

Opposite: Flight Lieutenant McCartney stands beside the artwork 'Relationships, Respect, Opportunities' that was unveiled during National Reconciliation Week 2020. ADF, foreign military and Australian Public Service personnel, as well as members from the Air Force Cadets, were encouraged to place their handprints on a piece of canvas as a visual representation of their connection to culture, country and community. (RAAF)

I love my work within the Air Force; I basically support the base commanders through the delivery of cultural expertise, liaising between the Air Force and First Nations communities. I maintain a personal rapport with the Elders in the local area as well as leaders and members of local communities. Most importantly, I advocate for the implementation of Defence's Reconciliation Action Plan and Our Place Our Skies, Air Force's Aboriginal and Torres Strait Islander Strategy.

My aim for my time in the Air Force is to continue to engage with local communities around the base, making sure they feel their voices are being heard and that we, as an organisation, are being culturally sensitive to their wishes in how we incorporate the everyday proceedings of the Air Force. This is becoming more evident, particularly with our ceremonies, that include Welcome to Country and Smoking Ceremonies, showing that our culture, the oldest in the world, is gradually being incorporated and recognised.

" *Receiving my Australian Defence Medal and having my service recognised has made me very proud not only for me but also for my family who have not easily been recognised for their service.* "

WILLIAM JOSEPH HAZEL

Service Number: A117528
Date of Birth: 17 February 1948
Place of Birth: Gin Gin, Queensland
Date of Enlistment: 5 May 1967
Date of Discharge: 3 July 1988
Rank: Corporal
Campaign: Vietnam

William Hazel, a Butchulla man, was born near Gin Gin in south-east Queensland. Prior to the arrival of Europeans, the area was occupied by people from the Gubbi Gubbi language group.

He left Nanango Public School at age 14, having completed Grade 8. He had attended nine schools during his childhood and, even though this did not actually reduce the amount of schooling he received, the constant change of teachers, standards and consistency between schools had a significant impact on his learning.

William applied to enlist in the Permanent Air Force (PAF) in 1967 at the age of 19. He worked as a labourer before enlisting. Two of his brothers were in the Australian Regular Army at the time and the security this offered influenced his decision to enlist, but he chose the Air Force over the Army. The impact of his early schooling made studying difficult for William; this was evident during his instructional and promotion courses, but he always persevered and never gave up. Instructors noted his willingness and determination to study. Interestingly, he never failed a practical or weapons handling test and became very proficient in the use of many weapons including grenades, claymores, shotguns, rifles and machine guns.

Above: Corporal Ken Triffitt and Leading Aircraftman 'Bill' Hazel on a transit flight, Nui Dat to Vung Tau, after celebrations at SAS Hill, South Vietnam, 1971. (RAAF)

Opposite: 'Bill' Hazel seated behind the twin M60 machine guns of a 'Bushranger' UH-1H Iroquois, South Vietnam, 1971. (RAAF)

William completed two tours of duty in Vietnam. The first was with No 2 Squadron, based at Phan Rang, from 14 February 1968 to 28 January 1969, on general Airfield Defence Guard (ADG) duties and was assessed as a 'thoroughly good all round ADG'. The second tour was to Base Support Flight Vietnam, from 28 January 1971 to 28 January 1972, but attached to No 9 Squadron as a gunner. During this tour, he flew numerous hours on a variety of missions. He was only posted for six months' duty but extended for another six months. A fellow member of the squadron remembered 'Billy' as a great mate, so reliable, dependable, good and gentle. In fact, he was so dependable that 'if you were under fire and Billy was on his gun, you knew your arse was covered'. He was also remembered for his wonderful, big moustache and his constant smile.

Above: 9 Squadron Iroquois Vietnam. (RAAF)

Opposite: No 1 Recruit Training Unit, Recruit Course 1615, 1981, of which 'Bill' was the instructor while posted to the unit. (RAAF)

If you were under fire and Billy was on his gun, you knew your arse was covered.

The squadron's activities in Vietnam varied from resupply of Army elements to the dangerous task of troop insertions and extractions. The gunship version of the Iroquois was developed in 1968 and included the addition of a six-barrel 7.62mm mini-gun and a rocket launcher, mounted forward and aft respectively per side, and two M60 machine guns mounted either side of the door openings.

There were limited opportunities for further growth in the ADG mustering, despite an organisational restructure recommended in 1978, so William eventually retired from the PAF in 1988 after 20 years of service.

ADAM SWAN

Date of Birth: 26 July 1971
Place of Birth: Parramatta, New South Wales
Date of Enlistment: 12 January 1993
Rank: Warrant Officer

It's important that my family see me serving proudly and hopefully making a difference. Military service has a clear connection with protecting your family and mob.

I was born in Parramatta and grew up in Macquarie Fields, New South Wales. My country is in and around Mudgee. I'm of the Wiradjuri people. It wasn't until my mum researched our family tree that we started to connect with our Indigenous heritage; the most inspiring part of this was learning about the life of my great-great-grandmother, who was known as Diana of Mudgee. She was taken in and raised by a white couple before going on to marry a white man.

I joined the Air Force in early 1993 after serving two years in the Army Reserve (artillery) and 11 years as a cadet and later officer in the Australian Air League (AAL). My family thought it was great my joining the Air Force, seeing it as an obvious extension of my time in the AAL. My only relative who served was my grandfather, Gordon Edward Swan, a staff sergeant in a Field Bakery Platoon during the Second World War. He survived the war, but unfortunately died in an industrial accident soon after.

Because of my time in the AAL, discipline, drill, and uniforms, etc., were second nature. The second part was the strong work ethic and good values my parents instilled in me. As a result, I was able to progress quickly through the ranks.

My initial postings were in warehousing followed by 15 years in Air Movements which involves the loading/unloading of transport aircraft, ground handling, cargo preparation

---

Opposite: Formal portrait of Adam Swan. (RAAF)

On the high ropes course with daughter Heidi. (Adam Swan)

and passenger handling. As a sergeant, I deployed three times to the Middle East and once to East Timor. Further postings included Movements training, Dangerous Goods training, Business Improvement Consultant (AFI), Safety Advisor, Squadron Warrant Officer, Movements Manager and, currently, Wing Warrant Officer. I've been posted to Richmond three times, as well as Tindal, Darwin, Wagga and Williamtown. I've been a warrant officer since 2009.

I'm the Wing Warrant Officer at No 42 Wing; my primary role is to advise the Officer Commanding (OC) on all matters affecting the enlisted workforce, including, welfare, discipline, morale, utilisation, training and preparedness. Additionally, I provide Senior Enlisted Leadership across the wing, enable the Wing Senior Enlisted Leadership Team (Warrant Officer Engineers and Squadron Warrant Officers), and assist the Commanding Officer/Executive Officer in the proper functioning of the Wing HQ.

As part of the command team with the OC, my aim is to ensure the wing achieves its mission of preparing for joint force airborne early warning and control, and intelligence, surveillance, reconnaissance and electronic warfare global operations. Our vision is to be the global benchmark for the provision of battlespace awareness, understanding and control. On a personal level, I want to help ensure our people enjoy their work in a cohesive team environment while being professionally rewarded. Staffing levels, competing priorities, concurrency of activity, retention of our 'best and brightest', and developing an employment proposition to meet contemporary expectations are my greatest challenges.

The opportunities I have had to broaden my outlook and profile have set me up for success in my current role. This included Instructing, AFI time and Safety Advisor, all separate jobs within the one career which pushed my boundaries and developed who I am today. Highlights included training at the University of Technology Sydney for the AFI job.

I've been fortunate to have many mentors. Warrant Officer Steve Wakeham was an excellent leader who understood how to get the best from people; he rarely raised his voice or had need to demonstrate anger, but he commanded respect by his professionalism, dedication and communication ability. Squadron Leader John DeHaan was similarly an excellent influence on me; he taught me to be bold in decision making and approach issues from a balanced perspective. Wing Commander Jason Taylor was a fine example of a true leader; we would have 'died in a ditch' for him, he genuinely cared about his people. I wish I could have been a better subordinate to him.

The Air Force has sent me to a variety of places outside of my progressive postings. I even met my wife in Baghdad! Soon after I enlisted, we were sent to fight the 1994 New South Wales bushfires. I remember one event at Winmalee when the fire front roared towards the houses we were attempting to protect with our 20-litre knapsack sprayers and fire rakes. We had no chance; we were only saved by quickly moving to the front of the houses (to shelter) as the fire came up, over and through the gaps between them. We wouldn't be placed in such a position these days.

During the Katherine floods in 1998, we witnessed a crocodile in the Shell garage and attempted to rescue kangaroos from the water. It rained for three days, then the sun came out; we all got sunburnt on top of three metres of water. The warehouse at the RAAF base became the supermarket for the whole town of Katherine; we had to escort people to stop hoarding.

All three deployments to the Middle East were great, working in Air Movements in the 1990s was great; we worked hard doing 24 hours on/24 hours off for two weeks, then having seven days off. This was real capability, we never had accidents.

During the Indian Ocean Tsunami response, I was the only senior at Air Movements section Darwin for the first five days. I led the small team to despatch a large number of aircraft in support of the relief operation. I didn't leave base for the whole time and found working in those extremely difficult circumstances greatly rewarding. For this work I received a Commander Combat Support Group Commendation.

The Australian Defence Force (ADF) provides an excellent foundation to your career; while some may only stay for their initial minimum period of service, others will go on to a rewarding long-term career. A benefit of service is the chance to have many careers within a career, as I mentioned through my experience as a Safety Advisor, Business Improvement Consultant and Instructor.

First Nations People are becoming more intrigued by what service may mean for them. The investment in attracting and recruiting First Nations People is slowly achieving results; retention is the bigger issue, but that affects the entire force, not just our mob. I think Air Force will continue to struggle to staff its capabilities going forward due to the competitive employment market and year-on-year erosion of conditions of service. I think we will largely meet non-technical recruiting targets but increasingly struggle to fill STEM, intelligence, cyber and security type jobs. There is great opportunity for young people to be trained while being paid.

It's important that my family see me serving proudly and hopefully making a difference. Military service has a clear connection with protecting your family and mob. I believe it's our responsibility to set a noble and strong example for our community and children. I struggled at school and, to be honest, didn't have outstanding prospects in terms of a meaningful career path. Joining the ADF gave me this; joining the Air Force gave me purpose and direction for which I'm very grateful. I am much more confident and outgoing, and I believe in my ability to achieve good outcomes for our people.

It hasn't all been so straightforward and uplifting. I suffer depression and anxiety as a result of my service. I have spent time in a mental health ward and have come back from the darkness and pain of a mental health condition. Every day is difficult, but I am stronger now than before. The Air Force has stood by me during the hardest days. The people you meet along the way, at every level, understand the life. I'm an introvert and most happy in my own company, but the chance to meet up with old mates on courses, deployments or postings is always a pleasure I look forward to.

The expectations of contemporary Air Force life are vastly different from when I joined, we had time for building teams, we had 'space' to try, fail and learn. However, as I like to say, it's a game of swings and roundabouts, work hard and make your own luck.

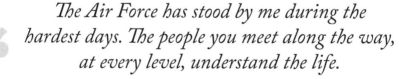

> *The Air Force has stood by me during the hardest days. The people you meet along the way, at every level, understand the life.*

Opposite Top: ANZAC Day 2014 at Lawson, New South Wales. (Adam Swan)

Opposite bottom: Adam and Louie, his French Bulldog. (Adam Swan)

SARAH WOODS

Date of Birth: 9 September 1979
Place of Birth: Ipswich, Queensland
Date of Enlistment: 27 March 2021
Rank: Flight Lieutenant

I aspire to develop and maintain enduring, genuine and impactful partnerships with Traditional Owners and the Air Force.

I am a proud Bundjalung woman of the Widjabul Wia bul clan, a direct descendant of King Jack Kapeen from the Northern Rivers region of New South Wales. My father, Warrant Officer Gary Woods, has served for 47 years in the Air Force. He signed up on 20 January 1975 as a Cook; the enlistment process was very different to the one I experienced. Growing up as an RAAF brat provided us with many great opportunities and experiences. We were fortunate to be posted all around Australia and even had the opportunity to live overseas with a posting to Butterworth in Malaysia. While my time with the Air Force, so far, has been short, my most memorable moment thus far has been serving at Amberley with my father.

I am currently on my first posting at No 23 Squadron, Amberley, having completed Officer Training School in 2021. As the Indigenous Liaison Officer for Amberley, my roles and responsibilities are to provide support and advice to the chain of command on Indigenous issues to enhance future Air Force capability through increased engagement with the Indigenous community, both externally and internally. This includes helping reduce the prejudice around First Nations peoples and their cultures, through increased awareness, education and participation.

I aspire to develop and maintain enduring, genuine and impactful partnerships with Traditional Owners and the Air Force throughout broader Queensland, acknowledging

Opposite: Flight Lieutenant Sarah Woods. (RAAF)

that their knowledge, skills and connection to country adds significant strategic value to the Air Force's capabilities. Personally, I look forward to continuing my education and growing my qualifications throughout my career.

Since serving at Amberley, I have been very fortunate to be a part of many community-led activities including the Murri Cup and the Elders Games. I have also had the opportunity to be involved in base-led community engagement activities. My most memorable to date was the Amberley NAIDOC Community Flight 2021; more than 130 Ipswich Aboriginal and Torres Strait Islander children and families experienced a flight in several military aircraft. Halfway through the flight, the ramps opened on the aircraft to reveal the view far below. Community engagement provides opportunities for the community to connect and experience a 'day in the RAAF'. This type of initiative is fundamental in strengthening the relationship between the local Aboriginal and Torres Strait Islander and Air Force communities. First Nations' cultures are heavily centred on coming together as one mob to share experiences, stories and culture. This gathering on, and flying over, country gives a new and shared experience of defending country. It gives both groups a shared story and common goal.

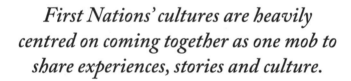

First Nations' cultures are heavily centred on coming together as one mob to share experiences, stories and culture.

Above: Flight Lieutenant Sarah Woods with her father, Warrant Officer Gary Woods. (RAAF)

Opposite: From left to right: Kelly Ryan, Tracey Thompson, Sarah Woods, Rhonda Purcell, Raymond Solinas, Nateesha Collins. (RAAF)

ARNOLD ALEXANDER LOCKYER

Service Number: 80471
Date of Birth: 4 May 1915
Place of Birth: Port Hedland, Western Australia
Date of Enlistment: 5 May 1942
Place of Enlistment: Perth, Western Australia
Date of Discharge: 21 August 1945 (killed while a prisoner of war)
Rank: Flight Sergeant
Campaign: Second World War

Arnold Alexander Lockyer, a Kariyarra Ngarluma man, was regarded as a gifted sportsman, fascinated by engine technology and possessed an excellent mechanical mind. According to his family, he reputedly knew how to fix anything.

Keen to fly, Arnold was nearly 27 when he applied to join the RAAF as aircrew in March 1942. Although he was assessed as intelligent with an understanding of internal combustion engines and mechanical experience, he lacked the required academic qualifications for aircrew. Subsequently, Arnold was enlisted as Ground Crew Trainee (Group V), with the rank of aircraftman class 1, and completed his enlistment on 5 May 1942 at No 4 Recruiting Centre in Perth, Western Australia.

Immediately after enlisting, Arnold proceeded to No 4 Recruit Depot where he attended No R156 Recruit Drill Course. This was followed by No 65 Trainee Group 2 Fitter Course at No 5 School of Technical Training in Perth. He then undertook training at No 242 Trainee Fitter Mechanical Course at No 1 Engineering School at Ascot Vale, Victoria, re-mustering to Flight Mechanic in November 1942. After further training on No 107 Fitter IIE Conversion Course conducted at the school, Arnold re-mustered to Fitter IIE. He was then posted to RAAF Pearce in Western Australia and to No 17 Repair and Salvage Unit (17RSU) at Cunderdin in April 1943 where he was reclassified as a leading aircraftman. The unit carried out repair and salvage operations on numerous aircraft types including Beauforts, Buffalos, Wirraways, Kittyhawks, Ansons and Hudsons. Continuing his training while still at 17RSU, Arnold successfully completed the Vultee Vengeance course, scoring a creditable 89 per cent.

Above: Formal portrait of Arnold Lockyer. (National Archives of Australia)

Opposite: Consolidated B-24L Liberator A72-92 of No 24 Squadron. It failed to return from a photographic reconnaissance mission to North Celebes on 27 July 1945. The aircraft was hit by Japanese anti-aircraft fire and crashed near Tomohon, North Sulawesi, in what is now Indonesia. (Jenny Scott)

However, Arnold did not give up his ambition to fly and, in November 1943, applied for transfer to aircrew. His persistence was finally rewarded and, on 4 July 1944, he was posted to No 3 Technical Air Gunners Course conducted at the Air Gunnery School at RAAF West Sale, Victoria. Arnold graduated in August 1944 and was then posted to No 7 Operational Unit at Tocumwal, New South Wales. This unit provided operational training for B-24 Liberator crews. Successfully completing the training, Arnold re-mustered as a Flight Engineer, was awarded the Flight Engineers Badge, and promoted to temporary sergeant.

In December 1944, Arnold was posted to the Heavy Bomber Replacement Training Unit, where he undertook further training on the Liberator. On completion of his training, he was posted to No 24 Squadron at Fenton Airfield, near Darwin in the Northern Territory. He joined the squadron as a Flight Engineer and top turret gunner on Liberators. In January 1945, the unit combined with Nos 21 and 23 Squadrons, also equipped with Liberators, to form the combat element of No 82 Wing. The three squadrons co-operated closely. In April, Nos 21 and 24 Squadrons contributed personnel and aircraft to form a detachment at Morotai and from there bombed the Japanese occupying forces and strategic targets on Borneo as a prelude to the Australian Army's amphibious assaults and capture of Borneo between May and July (Operation *Oboe*). Concurrently, the Liberators remaining at Fenton searched for, and attacked, shipping in the Timor, Banda and Arafura Seas.

Tragically, on 27 July, just 19 days before the end of hostilities, Arnold was Flight Engineer on Liberator A72-92 which failed to return from a sortie. Captained by Flight Lieutenant Kenneth J. Hanson of No 21 Squadron and crewed by No 21 Squadron personnel, plus Arnold and American weather observer Corporal John R. Waite, the aircraft was tasked with photographic reconnaissance over North Celebes. After it was reported missing, searching aircraft located the wreck of A72-92 about three kilometres south-west of Tomohon in the Manado area, North Celebes. It appeared to have struck the ground in a shallow dive.

It was later established that four of the 12 crew jumped from the stricken aircraft. Sergeant Charles N. Nichol did so without a parachute and was killed. The other three, one of whom was Arnold, were captured by the Japanese and taken to gaol at Kakaskasen near Tomohon. Sergeant John V. Orgill grabbed a bayonet and fought with his captors but was struck down and beaten to death.

On the morning of 21 August, six days after Emperor Hirohito declared the end of hostilities, but before the formal signing of surrender documents on 2 September, Arnold and Warrant Officer George G. Lindley were chloroformed and buried, probably alive, at Kaaten. Their bodies were later found intact and identified by dental checks. The other eight crew members were presumed to have died on 27 July.

Sergeant, later Flight Sergeant, Arnold A. Lockyer's body is interred at Ambon War Cemetery, Ambon, Maluku, Indonesia. He was survived by his wife Susanna Philomena and his three sons: Ronald, John and Samuel.

Crew of A72-92

Pilot F/Lt Kenneth John Hanson, 403585 (KIA) Roeville, NSW

Co-Pilot W/O Alfred Cook, 419295 (KIA) Spotswood, VIC

Crew Sgt Arnold Alexander Lockyer, 80471 (POW/KIA) Port Hedland, WA

Crew P/O George Grey Lindley, 427712 (POW/KIA) Mandurah, WA

Crew F/Sgt William James Maxwell, 435994 (KIA) Windsor, QLD

Crew F/Sgt Stephen Patrick Cloake, 441014 (KIA) Mitchelton, QLD

Crew F/O John James Oliver Hume, 427095 (KIA) Hilton, SA

Crew F/Sgt Frank Grainer Vincent Hutton, 437421 (KIA) Vale, VIC

Crew F/Sgt John Victor Orgill, 441469 (POW, beaten to death July 28 1945, MIA) East Fremantle, WA

Crew F/Sgt Brendan Michael Heslin, 440787 (KIA) Mendooran, NSW

Crew F/Sgt Charles Neville Nichol, 440381 (KIA) Sherwood, QLD

Observer Cpl John R. Waite, 36404344 USAAF, 15th Weather Squadron (KIA)

Liberator crews pose for a photo. (State Library Victoria, Argus Collection)

ANNIE SHEILA LOGAN

Service Number: 113419
Date of Birth: 2 October 1926
Place of Birth: Esperance, Western Australia
Date of Enlistment: 22 November 1944
Place of Enlistment: Perth, Western Australia
Date of Discharge: 16 January 1946
Rank: Aircraftwoman
Campaign: Second World War

Annie Logan was born in Esperance in late 1926, but was a resident of Cottesloe, a coastal suburb of Perth, with her family when, on 22 November 1944, she joined the Women's Auxiliary Australian Air Force (WAAAF). The Second World War had already been in progress for five years, almost the entirety of Annie's teenage years. She enlisted 'for the duration of the war plus twelve months' as a Cooks Assistant at No 4 Recruiting Centre, Perth, with the rank of aircraftwoman. Although it was just seven weeks after her 18th birthday, Annie was authorised to draw the adult rate of pay.

On enlistment, Annie was posted to No 3 WAAAF Depot in Karrinyup, Western Australia, to undertake Recruit Drill Course R41 along with 16 other recruits. The depot had been formed on 24 April 1942 with an authorised establishment of four officers, 40 airwomen and 100 trainees. At the time Annie arrived for training, there were 67 personnel on posted strength, including the recruits. Although the course kept recruits fully occupied, a wall newspaper and maps were maintained by the depot to keep recruits informed on topical subjects. Annie successfully completed the course on 20 December 1944, participating in the 'pass out' ceremony which was reviewed by the Staff Administrative Officer of Western Area.

Opposite: Enlistment photo of Annie Logan. (National Archives of Australia)

Immediately after recruit training, Annie was posted to RAAF Station Pearce, arriving there on 27 December; on 14 June 1945, she was posted to No 32 Radar Station. Located on Rottnest Island, 18 kilometres west of Fremantle, the radar station formed in the port in late 1942 before relocating to Rottnest by the end of that year. It was a fixed radar station tasked with monitoring aircraft movements and to provide early warning of enemy incursions. At the time of Annie's arrival, the island experienced possibly the wettest and stormiest month on record. Transport of personnel and the delivery of fresh rations to the island, the latter particularly welcomed by the nine RAAF and 18 WAAAF personnel on strength, was provided by No 7 Communication Unit.

Within two months of Annie's arrival, hostilities in the Pacific ended. On 4 January 1946, she was posted to No 5 Personnel Depot, located in Subiaco, for discharge.

Aircraftwoman Annie Logan discharged from the depot on 16 January 1946 and moved to Red Lake, Western Australia.

Above: Front entrance of Karrinyup golf club in Perth, used as No 3 WAAAF Depot. (Australian War Memorial)
Opposite: Trainee members of the WAAAF. (State Library Victoria, Argus Collection)

GRACE CASEY-MAUGHAN

Date of Birth: 22 March 1994
Place of Birth: Moruya, New South Wales
Date of Enlistment: 10 August 2018
Rank: Flight Lieutenant

" *... it felt incredible to be doing engagement the right way – developing strong and real relationships between the RAAF and the communities we serve.* "

I am an Ngarigo woman from the New South Wales Snowy Mountains. My mum is an Aboriginal woman and my dad is non-Indigenous.

I am not the first from my family to serve in the Defence Force. Both sides of my family, grandparents, uncles and aunts, and a cousin, have served in the Defence Force since the Second World War. I have maintained my family's commitment to serving Country, having joined the Air Force in August 2018 and taking up the role as an Indigenous Liaison Officer.

I completed my initial training at the Officer Training School in East Sale, Victoria, between August and December 2018. This training included 17 weeks of military management, leadership, military law, air power, ground defence, security, military skills, and Air Force values and ethics training. I graduated with five other Indigenous officers before taking up a position with the Chief of Staff's Branch at Air Force Headquarters in Canberra as an Indigenous Liaison Officer.

As newly commissioned Indigenous Liaison Officers, having the opportunity to serve on various Air Force bases and Defence establishments across Australia, our roles include building relationships with those local communities, promoting Indigenous recruitment and also promoting Aboriginal and Torres Strait Islander culture and programs within the Air Force.

Opposite: Flight Lieutenant Grace Casey-Maughan (left) and Squadron Leader Gary Oakley- in the backdrop, Mount Ainslie. (RAAF)

I can already look back and feel proud about what has been achieved in such a short period of time as an Indigenous Liaison Officer. Some of my most memorable moments include graduating from Officer Training School with my brothers and sisters as the first Indigenous Liaison Officers for the Air Force; taking part in community engagement activities, especially flying on a C-130 Hercules into Gilgandra and Lake Cargelligo, New South Wales, and, for the first time in Air Force's history, being officially 'Welcomed to Country'. Spending time with that mob on the ground and showing them the aircraft, it felt incredible to be doing engagement the right way – developing strong and real relationships between the Air Force and the communities we serve.

Something that will stay with me forever is conducting the reading at the 2019 Last Post Ceremony for Reconciliation Day at the Australian War Memorial. It was an honour to read the story of an Aboriginal man who served and died for his country. It was a freezing cold day in Canberra and we were expecting snow. I will always remember it.

In January 2021, I chose to change roles in the Air Force and become a Personnel Capability Officer. I now manage a small team of Personnel Capability Specialists as a part of Headquarters 41 Wing. My responsibilities revolve around the provision of human resources, administration, welfare support, command support, the management of unit finances, and management of Reserve personnel.

I aspire to continue to gain organisational experience and am hoping to deploy overseas and on exercises in the next couple of years. My near goal is to move into a Public Affairs Officer position. I think this role would afford me the opportunity to utilise my subject matter expertise and further promote Indigenous Affairs.

My longer-term goals are to use my degree in International Studies, perhaps in an overseas posting, or within the International Engagements Directorate.

Finally, with the sort of experiences and knowledge gained from such a broad spectrum of postings, I would like to return to where I began and reinvest my energy working in Air Force Indigenous Affairs.

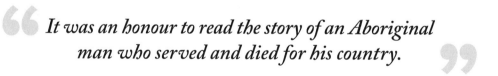

It was an honour to read the story of an Aboriginal man who served and died for his country.

Wing Commander Jonathon Lilley, Flight Lieutenant Grace Casey-Maughan and Flight Lieutenant Tjapukai Shaw at Gilgandra Aerodrome, NSW. (RAAF)

ERROL JONES INGRAM

Service Number: 424587
Date of Birth: 2 January 1924
Place of Birth: West Maitland, New South Wales
Date of Enlistment: 15 September 1942
Place of Enlistment: Sydney, New South Wales
Date of Discharge: 18 January 1946
Rank: Flying Officer
Campaign: Second World War

Errol was born in early January 1924 in West Maitland, New South Wales. When he decided it was his duty to enlist and do his part in the war, he chose to join the Army. He originally enlisted as a Sapper in May 1942 but decided the Air Force was for him instead, so discharged four months later and enlisted in the RAAF. Prior to joining up, Errol was studying to become a teacher.

After several courses and a promotion to leading aircraftman in February 1943, he commenced his flying training at No 8 Elementary Flying Training School, Narrandera, from March to June 1943. He then moved to No 5 Service Flying Training School, Uranquinty, where he was awarded his Flying Badge in August and promoted to sergeant the next day. He embarked for overseas service in November.

While training in the United Kingdom, Errol was promoted to flight sergeant and then commissioned on 7 November 1944, promoted to pilot officer the next day. Six months later, he was promoted to flying officer.

In the United Kingdom, he spent time at RAF Gamston, assigned to an operational training unit, before being posted to No 622 Squadron, No 3 Group. The squadron was a heavy bomber unit that was part of Bomber Command's main force from the summer of 1943 until the end of 1945. It was formed from C Flight of No 15 Squadron on 10 August 1943 and its Short Stirlings flew the unit's first operation the very same night. The squadron's records clearly show the higher risk of flying the Stirling at lower altitudes than the Lancasters and Halifaxes equipping other units.

The squadron flew 195 Stirling sorties on 41 raids, losing seven aircraft, a loss rate of 3.6 per cent. It converted to the Lancaster in December 1943, so the new type was used during some of the costly bombing campaigns in early 1944 and the squadron was not one of the units whose Lancaster loss figures are distorted by their late entry into service. It continued flying bombing raids as part of No 3 Group until April 1945 when it flew sorties for Operation *Manna*, dropping food supplies to the Dutch, and then repatriating prisoners of war to Britain as part of Operation *Exodus*.

Above: Enlistment photo of Errol Ingram. (National Archives of Australia)

Opposite: Operation *Exodus*: Aircrew brief released prisoners of war before the short flight back to the United Kingdom. At the end of the war, Bomber Command started flying to airfields in Western Europe to collect prisoners of war recently liberated from the camps. No 622 Squadron took part in these efforts. Errol is credited with taking part in six such flights. Source (RAAF)

In April, as the war in Europe was wrapping up, in an effort to alleviate the suffering of the starving Dutch, the Allies devised a plan to deliver much needed food via airlift. The Germans honoured their word, almost entirely, that they would not fire on the low-flying bombers, and countless Dutch civilians benefited from this 'manna from heaven'. From 29 April through to VE-Day, 8 May 1945, more than 5,500 sorties dropped over an estimated 10,000 tons of food.

At the height of the prisoner repatriation effort, aircraft were arriving in Europe at a rate of 16 per hour, bringing more than 1,000 people a day into British receiving camps. By the end of the operation, Allied forces had brought home more than 354,000 former prisoners of war.

After the end of the war in Europe, No 622 Squadron was used for troop transport flights between Italy and the UK, again bringing service personnel home, before being disbanded on 15 August 1945.

Errol returned to Australia where he discharged from No 2 Personnel Depot, Bradfield Park, on 18 January 1946.

Above: The crew of a bomber of No 622 Squadron RAF being debriefed by the intelligence officer at Mildenhall, Suffolk, after returning from a major raid on Berlin. (RAAF)

Opposite: From 29 April through to 8 May 1945, combined Allied efforts saw over 5,500 sorties dropping an estimated 10,000 tons of food for the starving and grateful Dutch. (Wikipedia)

GARY OAKLEY OAM

Date of Birth: 16 September 1953
Place of Birth: Katoomba, New South Wales
Date of Enlistment: July 1969
Rank: Squadron Leader

... given the low job prospects for an Indigenous boy in central New South Wales, I took my interests in the military to a new level ...

I was born in Katoomba in New South Wales' Blue Mountains. My people are the Gundungurra. I spent most of my youth in Katoomba, and later in Canowindra in central New South Wales, completing primary school at North Katoomba before moving on to Katoomba High School. I was always fascinated in military history and collected militaria but was particularly interested in becoming a baker. I was offered an apprenticeship as a pastry chef at the Hydro Majestic Hotel, but this fell through when my father was offered a job and the family moved to Canowindra.

I went back to high school after we moved but, given the low job prospects for an Indigenous boy in central New South Wales, I took my interests in the military to a new level, joining the Navy at 15. My initial training was at the Navy's shore training establishment at HMAS *Leeuwin* in Fremantle, Western Australia. I opted for employment as an Electrician and decided I may as well make a career out of the Navy for at least 20 years.

After eight years as an Electrician, I decided to change tack and was accepted into the Submarine Service, where I remained for 13 years. Unfortunately, this lifestyle took its toll on my health to the point where I decided to take on a new posting, relocating to Canberra to work in the Navy office, looking after sailors' personal and employment records.

I eventually transferred to the Australian Public Service (APS), working in an Indigenous military curatorial capacity at the Australian War Memorial (AWM); it was here that I was encouraged to look at joining the Air Force Reserves to work in the new Indigenous Affairs area. I transferred as a squadron leader and, while I kept working in the APS curatorial post with the AWM, I eventually resigned from the APS because I believed what the Air Force was doing was right for my people. Resigning from the APS meant I could devote more time and energy to the vital Indigenous Affairs role.

Opposite left: 1969 Junior recruits, HMAS *Leeuwin*. (Gary Oakley)

Opposite right: Gary at the Australian War Memorial when he was the Curator for Exhibitions. (Gary Oakley)

In 2019, I was awarded an Order of Australia Medal for my service to the Indigenous community through a range of organisations, including my time and service to the Air Force's Indigenous Affairs organisation as their Indigenous Historical Custodian. After six years in the custodian role, I had become aware of other opportunities where I could optimise my curatorial and historical expertise and transferred to the History and Heritage Branch in 2021.

In my current position with History and Heritage, I am responsible for actively assessing various Indigenous artefacts held on Air Force bases, continuing to engage with Indigenous communities (especially as matters are related to the Air Force), engaging with curators both domestically and overseas, and am currently collecting and researching the biographies of First Nations People who have served in the Air Force. I also currently serve as the National President of the Aboriginal & Torres Strait Islander Veterans & Services Association (ATSIVSA) and sit on several boards and committees as the First Nations representative in both Defence and non-defence groups.

There are many ways to protect country; putting on a uniform is one way that I have found that works for me.

Above: Opening night of the stage production *Black Diggers* at the Sydney Opera House. (Gary Oakley)

Opposite top: Leading the Anzac Day march in 2017. (Gary Oakley)

Opposite bottom: The ACT Families and Veterans Advisory Board of which Gary was a member. (Gary Oakley)

" *There are many ways to protect country;*
putting on a uniform is one way that
I have found that works for me. "

JAMES IAN MCLEOD

Service Number: A221431
Date of Birth: 1 September 1946
Place of Birth: Glen Innes, New South Wales
Date of Enlistment: 6 February 1962
Date of Discharge: 5 February 1982
Rank: Flight Sergeant
Campaign: Vietnam

James enlisted in the RAAF as an apprentice at the age of 15 years and five months, having just completed the New South Wales Intermediate Certificate examinations. One of the reasons he listed for joining was that his brother was a senior apprentice at the time and had apparently persuaded him to become one too. James enlisted as an Instrument Fitter Apprentice and attended the RAAF School of Technical Training at RAAF Base Wagga from February 1962 to July 1964 as part of No 16 Apprentice Intake. As an Instrument Fitter, James was taught to assemble and install precise instruments that measure, indicate, transmit, record and control various aspects of an aircraft's performance. He was required to fit and assemble instrument parts and check the instruments for accuracy and calibration to specifications.

After graduating at Wagga, James moved to RAAF Base Richmond for two consecutive postings. First, in August 1964, he was posted to No 36 Squadron, which was operating the C-130A Hercules, and, on 19 August 1966, he was posted to the similarly-equipped No 37 Squadron, which had re-formed earlier in the year. James was reclassified to leading aircraftman in July 1965 and promoted to corporal in July 1967, reflecting his consistently high evaluation reports.

James was next posted to No 1 Operational Conversion Unit at RAAF Base Amberley in Queensland on 29 April 1969. The unit's role was to convert pilots and navigators for operations on Canberra bombers in Vietnam. James himself was posted to serve with No 2 Squadron at Phan Rang in Vietnam, arriving on 21 May 1970. The squadron had a long and distinguished history beginning with its formation in Egypt in 1916 during the First World War. Subsequently disbanded and re-activated multiple times, during the Second World War the unit began with operating Ansons and Hudsons on maritime patrol and convoy escort duties off the Australian east coast. Later in the war, the squadron flew Beauforts (briefly) and Mitchells, attacking shipping and Japanese airfields. In 1958, No 2 Squadron re-equipped with Canberras after which it deployed to Butterworth in Malaysia as part of the British Commonwealth Far East Strategic Reserve.

In April 1967, the squadron was sent to Vietnam and commenced operations out of Phan Rang where it formed part of the United States Air Force's 35th Tactical Fighter Wing from April 1967 to June 1971. The squadron achieved 97 per cent serviceability rates and flew 4–6 per cent of the wing's missions but accounted for 16 per cent of the assessed bomb damage. James's role as a senior non-commissioned officer and instrument fitter played a significant part in the high rate of aircraft serviceability during his time with the squadron. On 1 November 1970, just six months after arriving in Phan Rang, he was promoted to sergeant. His posting at No 2 Squadron came to an end in April 1971, two months before the squadron also returned to Australia.

Opposite: Enlistment photo of James McLeod. (National Archives of Australia)

From Vietnam, James returned for a further posting with No 36 Squadron at Richmond. This was followed by a posting in 1973 to No 481 Squadron at RAAF Base Williamtown before, returning to Richmond a few months later to join No 2 Aircraft Depot. In 1974, he moved to No 486 Squadron, also at Richmond, and, in 1978, to Maintenance Squadron East Sale in Victoria. Shortly after arriving at East Sale, James was promoted to flight sergeant. As a senior non-commissioned officer, he was responsible for the activities and performance of a small team of similarly trained personnel. James remained at East Sale until 1982 when he returned to Richmond prior to discharge. During his career, James worked on C-130A and E-model Hercules, Winjeels, SP-2H Neptunes and Canberras. He was also reported as being very proficient in the maintenance of simulators.

Having completed 20 years' service in the Air Force, Flight Sergeant James McLeod discharged on 5 February 1982.

Top: Enlistment photo of James McLeod. (National Archives of Australia)
Bottom: No 2 Squadron barracks at Phan Rang in Vietnam. (RAAF)
Opposite: No 2 Squadron personnel in May 1971. (RAAF)

JAMES EVANS

Date of Birth: 12 May 1980
Place of Birth: Sydney, New South Wales
Date of Enlistment: 9 September 2014
Rank: Flying Officer

*... a mixture of hand gestures and relatively
calm actions eventually diffused the situation,
preventing the Iraqis from boarding the C-130.*

I was born in Sydney and am a proud Wiradjuri man currently living in Wagga Wagga with four beautiful children: Tayla, Brooklyn, Ruben and Hudson.

Prior to joining the Air Force, I gained numerous community experiences working for the local Aboriginal Medical Service, undertaking youth and men's health work. I coordinated several pre-employment programs and facilitated programs within correctional centres to decrease incarceration rates for Aboriginal and Torres Strait Islander men.

I enlisted in the Air Force on 9 September 2014 from Albury, New South Wales, and chose to become an Airfield Defence Guard (ADG). Essentially, ADGs are employed to provide security and defence of an Air Base, its people and assets. ADGs are also primarily involved in providing ground defence training, especially with respect to weapons training, and keeping Air Force personnel current on weapons.

After graduating from recruit and specialist ADG training, I was posted to RAAF Base Williamtown, near Newcastle, where I was actively involved in the security of Air Force assets, often conducting flight line security operations and working with patrol dogs. In the course of this posting, I participated in various exercises designed to maintain currency as an ADG at the highest levels so I was available to deploy at short notice. In those days, I was generally armed with the F88 Assault Rifle and the M9 Browning Pistol.

Despite deploying across Australia and occasionally overseas to provide support to both flight line and aircraft security operations, I don't think I was ever confronted with any significant threats. However, on one occasion, when I was in Iraq on flight line and aircraft security, I was required to challenge some Iraqis who were inadvertently looking to board Air Force aircraft. It was very challenging negotiating with these Iraqis, especially given we could not understand what each other was saying; a mixture of hand gestures and relatively calm actions eventually diffused the situation, preventing the Iraqis from boarding the C-130.

Opposite: Participating in a recruiting open day in Newcastle. (James Evans)

I've been involved in a range of domestic exercises including Op *Atlas*, as a part of the security operations involved in the Commonwealth Games, where a security force of 10,000 Queensland Police and Defence personnel ensured the safety of athletes, officials and spectators. As already mentioned, I've also deployed overseas, taking part in Operations *Manitou*, *Aslan*, *Okra* and *Highroad* where the focus was supporting operations in the Middle East with the ADGs providing full force protection to aircraft, aircrew, evacuees and essential equipment both in flight and on the ground within the confines of the respective airfield at the time.

Following my tour of duties overseas, I was posted to No 1 Recruit Training Unit (1RTU) in Wagga Wagga, New South Wales, the Air Force's initial entry training establishment for all non-commissioned personnel. At 1RTU, I was double hatted, being not only involved in providing mandatory weapon training to new recruits but also in coordinating the Indigenous Liaison position for RAAF Base Wagga.

In 2021, I was honoured to become an officer of the Personnel Capability Specialisation and, upon completion of training at Officer Training School in East Sale, Victoria, returned to Wagga and into No 31 Squadron as the full-time Indigenous Liaison Officer for RAAF Base Wagga.

Left: The Silver Commendation certificate received by James. (James Evans)

Right: James receiving the Silver Commendation from the Air Commander Australia. (RAAF)

This role has seen me provide base commanders, numerous recruits and trainees with cultural guidance, especially significant occasions which have given me an opportunity to promote First Nations culture and see how that has positively impacted personnel at RAAF Base Wagga. I am very keen to encourage First Nations People to join the Australian Defence Force (ADF); having come from the ranks and been commissioned has given me an opportunity to provide interested parties with a wholesome view of what the Air Force has to offer across the range of non-commissioned and commissioned roles.

In 2018, I represented the New South Wales RAAF Basketball team at the combined Defence Competition in Holsworthy and then, in 2020 and 2022, represented the ADF at the National Titles for Touch Football in Coffs Harbour.

In December 2021, I was recognised for my performance in the Indigenous Liaison Officer role, receiving a Silver Commendation from the Air Commander Australia. This award was presented for my efforts in coordinating cultural events, including those that complemented Air Force's Centenary activities, and in the implementation of cultural protocols for No 1 Recruit Training Unit while maintaining my primary responsibilities to provide specialist weapons training. It was an incredible honour, but I was really only doing my job to the best of my ability for my career, my Air Force, my people and country.

... I was really only doing my job to the best of my ability for my career, my Air Force, my people and country.

KEITH FARRELL

Service Number: 88048
Date of Birth: 9 June 1922
Place of Birth: Hobart, Tasmania
Date of Enlistment: 24 August 1942
Place of Enlistment: Hobart, Tasmania
Date of Discharge: 28 January 1946
Rank: Acting Sergeant
Campaign: Second World War

Keith Farrell was born in Hobart in mid-1922. Aged 20, on 24 August 1942 he enlisted for the duration of the Second World War plus 12 months in the Citizen Air Force, the active reserve component of the RAAF. Keith enlisted as a Trainee Group V with the rank of aircraftman class 1. At the time of his enlistment, he was employed as a draper's assistant. Prior to joining the RAAF, Keith had served for three and a half years with the Militia in the 40th Battalion. After enlisting at No 6 Recruiting Centre in Hobart, Keith proceeded immediately to No 1 Recruit Depot in Shepparton, Victoria, where he was one of 1,816 airmen arriving that month from various recruiting centres for training.

From Shepparton, Keith moved to No 4 School of Technical Training, where he completed No 105 Trainee Group II Fitter Course, before proceeding to the Armament School at Hamilton, Victoria. Keith graduated from No 39 Armourers Course on 22 January 1943. The next day, he was re-mustered to Armourer. After completing further training for this role, Keith proceeded to No 1 Service Flying Training School at Point Cook. While there, Keith reclassified to leading aircraftman.

In October, Keith was posted to No 3 Bombing and Gunnery School at RAAF West Sale, Victoria. The school had formed in January 1942 to provide gunnery training to air gunners, and bombing and gunnery training to air observers. On 9 December 1943, the school was renamed No 3 Air Gunnery School. On 18 October, Keith commenced training as an air gunner on No 38 (G) Course, from which he graduated a month later, qualifying for the Air Gunner Badge.

Opposite: Studio portrait of Keith Farrell as part of the Australian War Memorial's Reflections – Honouring Australian Second World War Veterans Project. (Australian War Memorial)

Keith was then posted to No 2 Flying Boat Repair Depot at Rathmines, New South Wales, effective from 19 November 1943. The depot had formed on 10 February 1943 and carried out repairs, overhauls and modifications to flying boats. On 28 January 1944, he was posted to No 3 Operational Training Unit (OTU), also based at Rathmines. The unit had formed almost two years earlier from the previous Seaplane Training Flight and provided operational training to new Catalina crews, while also conducting anti-submarine patrols. At the OTU, Keith undertook No 22 Operational Training Corporal Armourers Course. In June 1944, he was promoted to acting sergeant and aircrew as a flying boat air gunner.

On 9 August, Keith joined No 42 Squadron which was based at Melville Bay, Northern Territory, and operating Consolidated Catalina flying boats. The squadron had formed in Darwin in June 1944 before moving to Melville Bay. Keith arrived as the squadron was building up ahead of commencing operations on 27 August. It joined Nos 11, 20 and 43 Squadrons in carrying out mine-laying operations. These units laid sea mines in the Straits of Banka, Lambeth, Tiworo, Boeteng and Wowoni in the Celebes, followed by similar operations in Makasar Harbour and Pare Pare Bay. During 1945, mining operations extended to the Chinese coast and Formosa and Sumatra.

In addition to mine laying, No 42 Squadron was also tasked with searching for and striking enemy shipping. Hostilities in the Pacific ended on 15 August 1945, after which the squadron helped repatriate liberated prisoners of war from Manila and time-expired personnel from Labuan. During offensive operations, which lasted about a year, the squadron laid 549 mines and dropped 17 tons of bombs during a total of 5,270 operational hours.

Keith's operational tour with the squadron concluded on 9 May 1945 and encompassed 14 strikes and attacks. He accumulated 241 hours and 20 minutes during operations at night and 151 hours and 20 minutes in daylight. On 21 January 1946, Keith, who had now reverted to his substantive rank of leading aircraftman, reported to No 6 Personnel Depot in Hobart for discharge.

Leading Aircraftman Keith Farrell discharged from the RAAF in Hobart on 28 January 1946.

Top: No 42 Squadron Catalina. (State Library Victoria, Argus Collection)
Bottom: Militia unit on parade. (State Library Victoria, Argus Collection)
Opposite: Enlistment photo of Keith Farrell. (National Australian of Archives)

LINDA LESTER

Service Number:	174865
Date of Birth:	18 January 1921
Place of Birth:	Granite Downs, South Australia
Date of Enlistment:	23 April 1945
Place of Enlistment:	Melbourne, Victoria
Date of Discharge:	28 March 1947
Rank:	Aircraftwoman
Campaign:	Second World War

Linda was born at Granite Downs, in north-west South Australia, in 1921. With her brothers and sisters, she was raised at the Colebrook Home for Aboriginal Children. She was the first child from the home to receive her qualifying certificate and graduate from Quorn Primary School in 1934. For a time, she worked at Colebrook helping new children to settle in.

Linda joined the Women's Auxiliary Australian Air Force (WAAAF) on 23 April 1945 at No 1 Recruit Centre, Melbourne, Victoria, as a Sick Quarters Attendant; she was 24 years old. She had already been nursing for four years and was employed by the Salvation Army. The recruit centre was formed on 7 September 1939 at Latrobe Street, Melbourne, and subsequently disbanded in October 1945. During this time, it recruited 48,430 ground staff, 13,128 aircrew and 6,541 WAAAFs.

Linda was sent to No 1 WAAAF Training Depot in April 1945. On completion of her training, she went to the Medical Training Unit, Preston, Victoria. While there are no courses listed on her file, the unit was responsible for courses on the instruction of hygiene inspectors, medical officers, medical orderlies, nursing orderlies, RAAF nurses and clerk medical assistants.

Above: Heidelberg Military Hospital, Victoria. (State Library Victoria)

Opposite: WAAAFs on parade. (State Library of South Australia)

Linda was then posted to No 1 Wireless Air Gunners School, Ballarat, for six months, No 1 Air Ground Radio School, Ballarat, for 12 months, and No 1 Radio Installation and Maintenance Unit, Melbourne, for three months. She served at No 6 RAAF Hospital, a lodger unit at Heidelberg Repatriation Hospital, from 11 February 1946 until her discharge in March 1947. The hospital began service as a section of the Army's 115th Australian General Hospital at Heidelberg in Melbourne, providing care and rehabilitation for servicemen returned from active service overseas. It relocated to RAAF Base Laverton on 23 May 1949.

Heidelberg served as a training hospital and its care and management of war injuries and trauma was recognised to be among the most advanced in the country. The staff at Heidelberg changed constantly during the war, but there was always a core of staff in the wards that had experienced front-line action in the Second World War. In May 1947, the hospital was handed over to the Repatriation Commission to create the Repatriation General Hospital Heidelberg. It provided medical treatment for eligible ex-servicemen and women and, if space allowed, their families. A large portion of the staff that joined the new hospital had served in medical and combat units. The shared experience of war between staff and patients greatly contributed to the type of care that was provided at the hospital. Ex-service nursing staff continued to work in the hospital until the late 1970s, instilling a patient-focused ethos into those they trained.

Linda met her husband while working at the Heidelberg Repatriation Hospital after the war. She and her sister Nellie married Vincent and James Nihill respectively. Linda worked at Heidelberg Repatriation Hospital and Macleod Repatriation Hospital for 36 years.

Opposite top: A new member of the WAAAF being kitted out with uniforms on enlistment. (Mitchell Library, State Library of New South Wales)

Bottom: Enlistment Photo of Linda Lester. (National Archives of Australia)

MELISSA MILLER

Date of Birth: 6 April 1973
Place of Birth: Prahran, Victoria
Date of Enlistment: 13 April 2004
Rank: Flight Lieutenant

 Life in the RAAF is hectic at times, rewarding and lots of opportunities both here and abroad.

I am a Jardwadjali (Jadawadjali) woman from Horsham in Victoria. I believe I may be the first member of my family, that I am aware of, to have served within the Australian Defence Force. Although I am still trying to trace my family history to ascertain if any members have served, it has proven somewhat difficult to date but I will continue my investigations.

I previously served in the Royal Australian Navy, joining in April 1994 as an Underwater Controller, trained in the Mulloka sonar system, which is now known as a Combat Systems Operator. I had postings to HMAS *Cerberus*, HMAS *Watson*, HMAS *Tobruk* and HMAS *Newcastle*.

Having previously served in the Navy, in April 2004, I decided to make the switch and joined the RAAF as a Non-Commissioned Officer, Air Surveillance Operator. On completion of training at RAAF Edinburgh and RAAF Williamtown, I was posted back to Edinburgh to No 1 Radar Surveillance Unit, now called No 1 Remote Sensor Unit. While at the unit, I started studying a nursing degree, before deciding a career change was in order, and then, in 2007, I became a Military Skills Instructor with postings to No 1 Recruit Training Unit at Edinburgh before the school moved to RAAF Base Wagga.

Opposite: Flight Lieutenant Melissa Miller. (Melissa Miller)

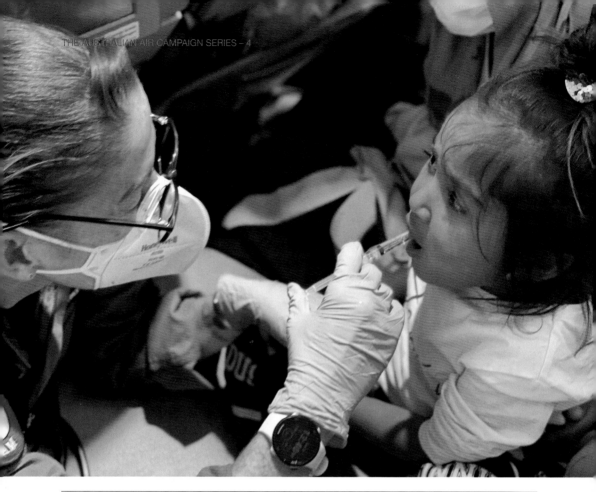

Flight Lieutenant Melissa Miller administering aid during a recent deployment. (RAAF)

My time as a Military Skills Instructor was extremely rewarding; watching the changes of the young men and women who have enlisted in the Defence Force and having input into their success and career was very satisfying. I have deployed on multiple exercises in various roles and operations, both in Australia and overseas, with each and every one different, which gives a new perspective on so many things. We are very fortunate to be able to receive these opportunities within the ADF.

While undertaking the role of a Military Skills Instructor at Wagga, I went to the officer selection board and was successful. I was commissioned and gained entry into the Civil School Scheme, where I went to Charles Sturt University, Wagga Wagga, to undertake a Bachelor of Nursing, which I completed in 2011. On graduation, I then completed two years of post-graduate studies with the Royal District Nursing Services in Melbourne. I was then posted back as a Nursing Officer to RAAF Williamtown. At the end of 2014, I was posted to RAAF Base Richmond at No 1 Expeditionary Health Squadron (1EHS) Detachment Richmond, with an attachment to No 3 Aeromedical Evacuation Squadron (3AMES). I then moved to 2EHS Williamtown for a few years and, in 2021, I was posted back to 3AMES Richmond, where I am currently serving.

My current role as an Operations Officer (OPSO)/Nursing Officer at 3AMES sees us conducting all of the Australian Defence Force's Aeromedical Evacuations both in Australia and overseas, including all operations and exercises. It's a unique unit and we are able to work with fixed or rotary-wing aircraft and utilise either civilian or military aircraft in order to return a member to their home location. My role is very unique in that 3AMES does not have a specialised OPSO as the OPSO; it has always been a clinician, either a Nursing Officer or Medical Officer, because clinical decisions need to be made in order to make sure the right person and/or team is tasked with the job. It's a big challenge with a small staff of highly skilled personnel, especially if you have multiple, concurrent aeromedical evacuations missions while also being available 24/7 to answer the calls to get a team ready to go.

One of my biggest personal achievements, to date, was receiving the Major Gregory John 'Frenchie' McDougall Memorial Award from the ADF Basketball Association. It is awarded by previous recipients, encompasses the mateship and friendships that are developed through sport, and was voted on by my peers. It is for those who have contributed in all aspects, both socially on and off the court, and also contributed to improving and encouraging new members to be actively involved.

I was fortunate to undertake the female Indigenous Liaison Officer's role for Exercise *Kummundoo*. This is the RAAF's contribution to remote communities for the National Aboriginal Community Controlled Health Organisation's dental program. I was involved in attending schools and health facilities to educate the next generation on health and the ADF's career opportunities. During this time, I also utilised my nursing background to assist and work in remote health facilities. It's tasks like these that make life in the Royal Australian Air Force so rewarding.

... watching the changes of the young men and women who have enlisted in the Defence Force and having input into their success and career was very satisfying.

MYRTLE HARRIS

Service Number: 111864
Date of Birth: 26 June 1921
Place of Birth: Northam, Western Australia
Date of Enlistment: 17 November 1943
Place of Enlistment: Perth, Western Australia
Date of Discharge: 1 March 1946
Rank: Aircraftwoman 1
Campaign: Second World War

Myrtle Harris was born on 26 June 1921 in Northam, Western Australia. On 3 December 1942, aged 21 and a half, Myrtle applied for enrolment as an airwoman in the Women's Auxiliary Australian Air Force (WAAAF) as a Trainee Telegraphist. She was found to be unsuitable for the role and her application did not proceed. She applied again in September 1943, this time seeking to enlist as a Trainee Technical. On the application she recorded her occupation as nursery maid. Undergoing the relevant trade test, she did not meet the entry requirements for the Trainee Technical category but was found suitable for entry as an Aircraft Hand.

Accordingly, on 17 November 1943, then 22, Myrtle reported to No 4 Recruiting Centre in Perth where she enlisted in the WAAAF as an Aircraft Hand for the duration of the war plus 12 months. From the recruiting centre, she proceeded immediately to No 3 WAAAF Depot along with 23 other recruits. The depot had formed on 24 April 1942 and provided recruit and drill training to new entrants as well as trade training to WAAAF signal clerks and mess stewards. It disbanded on 23 March 1945, having trained 1,417 WAAAF recruits.

Myrtle successfully completed No R25 Recruit Drill Course in December 1943. Her first posting after recruit training was to No 4 Service Flying Training School at Geraldton, Western Australia. The school had formed at Geraldton on 10 February 1941 to provide intermediate and advanced flying training for pilots as part of the Empire Air Training

Opposite: Enlistment photo of Myrtle Harris. (National Archives of Australia)

Scheme. The school continued to operate until early 1945 and ceased to function on 31 May of that year. In early May 1945, hostilities had ended in Europe and the end of the war in the Pacific was a less than four months away. Myrtle remained at the school throughout 1944 and was joined there by her sister Ruby in November. Both posted out in March 1945 as the school's personnel numbers shrank ahead of its disbandment.

On 21 March, Myrtle commenced duty at No 7 Communication Unit at Guildford, about 13 kilometres north-east of Perth. The unit had originally formed at RAAF Pearce on 24 November 1943 and moved to Guildford in November 1944. It provided communications and aerial towing, aerial target towing and special duties. In March, when Myrtle arrived, among several aircraft types operated by the unit were Avro Ansons and Tiger Moths used for transport flights and Vultee Vengeances for target towing. Aerial targets were towed in support of anti-aircraft artillery training for both Army units and Royal Australian Navy ships, and for air-to-air gunnery practice by RAAF squadrons. The unit also carried out meteorological flights in a Wirraway. It achieved 699 flying hours in March.

Myrtle's stay at Guildford came to an end on 4 April when she was posted to No 4 Central Recovery Depot at Maylands, Western Australia. On arrival at Maylands, Myrtle was barracked by No 4 Stores Depot, with 11 other WAAAFs, at 'The Gables', a large home in the area. All other personnel lived out. Morale and welfare were enhanced by sport and parties organised during stand-down periods.

After two months at Maylands, Myrtle moved again to RAAF Station Pearce on 11 June, arriving with Ruby. It was the sisters' final posting. On 14 February 1946, Myrtle proceeded to No 5 Personnel Depot for discharge, which she completed on 1 March, five days before her younger sister. Ruby had followed in Myrtle's footsteps by enlisting in the WAAAF as an Aircraft Hand in July 1944. The sisters also had a brother, David, who served in the Army.

Left: A member of the WAAAF conducting aircraft instrument checks. (State Library Victoria, Argus Collection)
Right: Women's Auxiliary Australian Air Force members salute during a parade. (State Library Victoria, Argus Collection)
Opposite: Members of the WAAAF working on the wing of a Catalina flying boat. (State Library Victoria, Argus Collection)

ROY HILL

Service Number: 427382
Date of Birth: 25 August 1913
Place of Birth: Busselton, Western Australia
Date of Enlistment: 6 July 1942
Place of Enlistment: Perth, Western Australia
Date of Discharge: 18 February 1946
Rank: Flying Officer
Campaign: Second World War

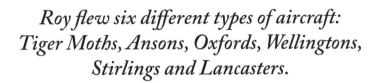

> *Roy flew six different types of aircraft: Tiger Moths, Ansons, Oxfords, Wellingtons, Stirlings and Lancasters.*

Roy Hill was born in Busselton, Western Australia, in August 1913. At the age of 28, he joined the Citizen Air Force at No 4 Recruiting Centre in Perth. The RAAF consisted of two branches: the Permanent Air Force and the Citizen Air Force, a forerunner of today's RAAF Active Reserve. Roy enlisted under the Empire Air Training Scheme as an aircrew trainee with the rank of aircraftman 2nd class. At the time of his enlistment, Roy was a miner living in Norseman with his wife, Gladys Edith Hill.

Roy spent the next 21 months undergoing training in Australia, commencing with the Recruit Drill Course, between 6 and 27 July 1942, at No 4 Recruit Depot in Busselton. He then proceeded immediately to No 9 Elementary Flying Training School at Cunderdin for basic flying training on Tiger Moths, followed by further training at No 5 Initial Training School at Clontarf, after which he was among 32 aircrew trainees on No 32 Course to be categorised as Pilot (out of the 58 who commenced training). Following categorisation, on 1 December 1942 Roy remustered to Leading Aircraftman II (P). Still in Western Australia, he then moved to the next stage of training, at No 4 Service Flying Training School, Geraldton where he underwent more advanced flying instruction on twin-engine Avro Ansons. Roy was awarded the Flying Badge (his wings) on 25 June 1943 and was promoted to temporary sergeant.

Destined for service overseas, at various times between March and August 1943 Roy proceeded to Nos 5, 1 and 2 Embarkation Depots, respectively located at Subiaco, Ascot Vale in Victoria, and Bradfield Park in New South Wales. At the time, the role of the embarkation depots was to house and prepare personnel for embarkation to overseas posts. At these depots, personnel were kitted, equipped, medically examined, vaccinated, inoculated and received any required dental treatment ahead of their voyage.

Roy set sail from Sydney on 11 August and disembarked in England on 9 October 1943. On the day after disembarking, he was processed through the RAAF's No 11 Personnel Despatch and Receiving Centre at Bournemouth, Sussex. This unit was the receiving station for RAAF non-commissioned aircrew arriving in the United Kingdom. With effect from the day of his arrival, Roy was attached to the Royal Air Force. Roy was promoted to temporary flight sergeant and proceeded to undertake various operational flying training courses with RAF units.

Opposite: Pilot trainees awaiting their turn for training on de Havilland Tiger Moth aircraft. (State Library Victoria, Argus Collection)

In February 1944, Roy commenced training at No 20 (P) Advanced Flying Training Unit at Kidlington, Oxfordshire, and trained at No 1538 Beam Approach Training Flight at Croughton, in West Northamptonshire, on twin-engine Airspeed Oxfords. He then proceeded to No 29 Operational Training Unit at North Luffenham, Rutland, for training on twin-engine Vickers Wellington bombers. Further work followed at No 1660 Heavy Conversion Unit at Swinderby, Lincolnshire, where he converted to the Short Stirling four-engine heavy bomber. Roy was granted a commission as a pilot officer on 2 November and commenced duty at No 5 Lancaster Finishing School at Syerston, Nottinghamshire.

The many months of training finally came to an end on 12 February 1945 when Roy was posted to No 106 Squadron at Metheringham in Lincolnshire, a unit formerly commanded by Guy Gibson in 1942 (he went on to lead the famous Dam Buster raid in May 1943). Roy was then posted to No 189 Squadron, another Lancaster unit based at Bardney, Lincolnshire. Hostilities in Europe came to an end and Roy's operational flying ended on 11 June 1945. Both squadrons were involved in the repatriation of prisoners of war after the cessation of hostilities in Europe. Since commencing operations, Roy had flown 11 sorties over a combined 80.15 flying hours. He was promoted to flying officer on 2 May.

After the end of the war in Europe, the repatriation and demobilisation of RAAF members posted overseas proceeded quickly. Following about two months at sea, Roy disembarked from the *Aquitania* at Fremantle, Western Australia, on 22 November 1945. He was one of 213 Western Australian and 229 South Australian RAAF members aboard. On disembarking, he was taken to No 5 Personnel Depot for discharge. During his RAAF career, Roy flew six different types of aircraft: Tiger Moths, Ansons, Oxfords, Wellingtons, Stirlings and Lancasters.

Roy also had two other brothers who served during the Second World War. Lance Corporal John Hill was with the 2/4 Machine Gun Battalion. He sadly died of dysentery at Changi, Singapore, on 11 March 1943. Roy's other brother joined the Navy. During his service, Able Seaman Hill was also captured by the Japanese after his ship, HMAS *Perth*, was sunk in the Battle of Sunda Strait in 1942; he spent the remainder of the war as a prisoner of war.

Flying Officer Roy Hill discharged from the Royal Australian Air Force on 18 February 1946.

Opposite top: Roy took part in 11 operations over Germany and Occupied Europe. On the night of 25 April 1945, Roy and his crew took part in Bomber Command's final heavy bomber raid, to the Vallo fuel refinery in Tønsberg, Norway. This image shows the results of the operation some 12 hours later. (RAAF)

Opposite bottom: No 106 Squadron Lancaster (Roy's unit). In the foreground is a 4,000-pound High-Capacity bomb as used on numerous targets in Germany. (RAAF)

DONALD TAYLOR

Date of Birth:	9 January 1960
Place of Birth:	Cloncurry, Queensland
Date of Enlistment:	10 December 1979
Place of Enlistment:	Townsville, Queensland
Rank:	Warrant Officer

Donald Taylor is a proud descendant of the Kalkadoon and Ngawun/Yirendali people, from north-west Queensland. In what is often regarded as the 'Friendly Heart of the Great North-West of Queensland', Donald spent most of his youth growing up between Cloncurry and Julia Creek.

Growing up in Julia Creek provided opportunities to develop and uphold community values. Social interaction was achieved through community festivities such as music and sporting events. 'I joined the local Boy Scouts and embraced the Scouts' Promise and motto "Be Prepared" and, over the Christmas holidays in 1974–75, I attended the 7th International Jamboree at Tokoroa in New Zealand.'

Then, in 1976, Donald attended All Souls School for Boys which was established by the Bush Brotherhood of St Barnabas in 1920 as a memorial school to the fallen of the First World War. The school provided an Army Cadets Program where Donald recalled, 'I learnt skills such as drill, field craft, first aid, navigation and leadership, ending with a term bivouac for two weeks at Sellheim Army Camp on the Burdekin River in Far North Queensland.'

With a number of his uncles serving in the Army during the Second World War, including his father who was conscripted to the Army under the National Service Act in 1953, like many members from his community, the military was no stranger to Donald's family and, as he grew up, there was a compelling sense of loyalty to protect Australia and his homeland.

Looking back at other factors that would eventually convince Donald service life was something he would pursue, the story of America's black aviators, particularly that of the Tuskegee Airmen and their success in the military, especially their acceptance within the wartime Army Air Forces and the post-war United States Air Force, would provide convincing reasons for him to think seriously about joining the Air Force. Following on from his father's military service, Donald's interest in the military came to fruition when he joined the Royal Australian Air Force on 10 December 1979.

While still serving, the now Warrant Officer Donald Taylor can look back on a long and successful career in both Permanent Air Force and (current) Reserve capacities spanning more than 40 years. Having started as a Motor Transport Fitter after completing initial trade training at the RAAF School of Technical Training in Wagga Wagga, New South Wales, Donald is now at the top of his trade serving in Joint Logistics Command as the Trade Repair Officer working out of RAAF Base Amberley in Queensland.

Left: Left to right Group Captain Lisa Jackson Pulver, Warrant Officer Donald Taylor, RAAF Elder Harry Allie. (RAAF)

'*You never stopped learning, the capacity to learn is a gift; the ability to learn is a skill; the willingness to learn is a choice.*'

Among his career highlights, Donald spent time at the RAAF School of Fire and Security as a trade instructor for maintenance and operations of the Air Force's Airfield Fire Fighting Vehicles. The significance of this instruction was that it provided relevant Air Force personnel with the wherewithal to conduct crucial firefighting and rescue services, especially in the event of aircraft accidents.

Working within the aviation ground maintenance area, Donald would see various postings to New South Wales, Queensland and the Northern Territory, where, upon promotion to sergeant, he would become highly proficient in the storage and handling of aviation fuels.

Moving into the Air Force's Expeditionary Force, responsible for providing combat support to deployed Air Force elements, Donald's achievements were rewarded with him being promoted to warrant officer and appointed as the Squadron Warrant Officer for No 382 Expeditionary Combat Support Squadron in 2013. Later, he deployed to No 19 Squadron, Royal Malaysian Air Force, Butterworth, as Officer-In-Charge Mechanical Equipment and Operations Maintenance Section and then saw out two further deployments to the Middle East Area of Operations.

Other career highlights include his appointment as the inaugural Senior Enlisted Adviser of Indigenous Affairs, a role that actively supported programs to recruit Aboriginal and Torres Strait Islander people into Defence, improve retention, and promote diverse and culturally appropriate workplaces.

While this appointment came later in his career, it recognised the many years Donald had already advocated for First Nations Peoples to look at careers in Defence, including the benefits of remaining at school and obtaining better grades that would ideally lead to better opportunities and options in life.

Making the most of opportunities and being the best you could be are Donald's mantra for First Nations People, and in his view 'you never stopped learning, the capacity to learn is a gift; the ability to learn is a skill; the willingness to learn is a choice.'

... there was a compelling sense of loyalty to protect Australia and his homeland.

Opposite Page: Left to right Flight Sergeant Brett West and Flight Sergeant Donald Taylor Middle East Area of Operations. (RAAF)

Above: Flight Sergeant Donald Taylor. (RAAF)

RUBY HARRIS

Service Number: 113264
Date of Birth: 14 August 1925
Place of Birth: Toodyay, Western Australia
Date of Enlistment: 5 July 1944
Place of Enlistment: Perth, Western Australia
Date of Discharge: 6 March 1946
Rank: Aircraftwoman 1
Campaign: Second World War

Ruby Harris was born in Toodyay, Western Australia in August 1925. On 31 May 1944, three months short of her 19th birthday, she applied to enlist in the Women's Auxiliary Australian Air Force (WAAAF) as an Aircraft Hand. As noted on her application, she was fully conversant with the duties associated with this mustering as, six months earlier, her older sister, Myrtle, had enlisted in the same role. At the time of her application, Ruby was unemployed and was undoubtedly pleased when she was notified to present at No 4 Recruiting Centre in Perth to complete her enlistment. She did so on 5 July 1944, enlisting for the duration of the war plus 12 months. Ruby was five weeks short of turning 19 and was to follow a similar career path to her sister.

Immediately after enlisting at No 4 Recruiting Centre, Aircraftwoman Ruby Harris proceeded to No 3 WAAAF Depot along with 32 other WAAAF recruits. Just as her older sister Myrtle had done earlier, Ruby underwent basic recruit and drill training before moving on to her trade training that would familiarise her with the role of an Aircraft Hand. Like her sister, Ruby would successfully complete her Recruit Drill Course on 2 August 1944, nine months later, and also have her passing out parade reviewed by the Senior Air Staff Officer of Western Area.

Following on in her sisters footsteps, Ruby's first posting after recruit training was to No 7 Communication Unit at Guildford to the north-east of Perth. At that time it continued to provide communication services, and aerial target towing. Ruby reported for duty on 5 August 1944, where the unit was still based at Pearce using Avro Ansons and Tiger Moths for communications flights, and transporting personnel and Vultee Vengeances, previously dive bombers, for towing targets.

Above: WAAAF Recruits on the Drill Square during training. (Mitchell Library, State Library of New South Wales)
Opposite: WAAAF Aircraft Hands walk past a Lockheed Hudson on the flight line. (State Library Victoria, Argus Collection)

After a stay of three months at Pearce, Ruby was posted to No 4 Service Flying Training School at Geraldton, Western Australia, with effect from 17 November 1944, joining her sister Myrtle who had arrived at the School in January. For Ruby and her sister Myrtle they would remain at the School until March, increasingly seeing units such as No 4 Service Flying Training School shrinking ahead of their disbandment.

On 21 March 1945, Ruby posted into No 4 Central Recovery Depot at Maylands, a suburb of Perth and was accommodated in a large house called 'The Gables', with 11 other WAAAFs. While the war was drawing to an end, good accommodation, sporting activities and parties helped to keep spirits high when not on duty.

Ruby's stay at Maylands lasted less than three months as, on 11 June, she returned to RAAF Pearce, arriving at the same time as Myrtle. It was their final posting. On 14 February 1946, Ruby proceeded to No 5 Personnel Depot for discharge. While Ruby and Myrtle had both served in the Air Force, their brother David, had served in the Army.

Aircraftwoman Ruby Harris discharged from the WAAAF at No 5 Personnel Depot on 6 March 1946.

Above: Enlistment photo of Ruby Harris. (National Archives of Australia)

Opposite: Members of the WAAAF fitting bomb racks to an Airspeed Oxford. (State Library Victoria, Argus Collection)

STEPHEN FRANCIS WEAVER AM

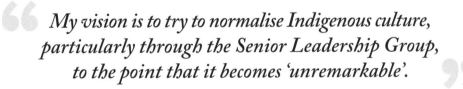

Date of Birth: 6 July 1966
Place of Birth: Gundagai, New South Wales
Date of Enlistment: 4 November 1987
Rank: Warrant Officer

> *My vision is to try to normalise Indigenous culture, particularly through the Senior Leadership Group, to the point that it becomes 'unremarkable'.*

I was born in Gundagai in central New South Wales and am a proud Wiradjuri man. I spent my childhood in Gundagai, finding my interests gravitating towards activities outside the classroom. This would have a strong bearing on my eventual Air Force career.

The classroom was challenging. I found myself inside the classroom, always looking outside and was often berated by the teachers as a result. This was quickly made up for when it came to sport. I enjoyed many sports, so much so that I became captain of the football and swimming clubs, enjoying the responsibilities of leadership as much as the physicality.

While drawn to the military in terms of my appreciation and admiration for service and sacrifice, I remember watching in awe as a Catafalque Party performed its drill during an Anzac Day ceremony in Gundagai. A good mate subsequently strongly recommended Service life, which ultimately convinced me to join the Defence Force. I joined the Air Force in November 1987.

Opposite: On operations in the Middle East in 2011. (Stephen Weaver)

" *I remember watching in awe as a Catafalque Party performed its drill during an Anzac Day ceremony in Gundagai.* "

I graduated from recruit training at the top of my class. I then undertook specialist trade training as a Supplier, essentially looking after all manner of Air Force logistics. However, after eight years in the role, I yearned for a trade that would match my interests in physicality, opting to become a Physical Training Instructor (PTI).

After 12 months of preparatory training, including learning about the body's physiology and then being assessed for suitability to undertake PTI training at HMAS *Cerberus*' gruelling assessment week, a real test of physical and mental resilience, I was recommended for training as a PTI, eventually graduating with the Student of Merit award. I have subsequently been posted to various bases including Wagga, the Air Force's home of technical training, Tindal in the Northern Territory, and Amberley in Queensland. Being a PTI is much more than just leading an exercise session to make people fit. We are responsible for instructing on military self-defence (a type of hand-to-hand combat), developing our troops' resilience, and keeping them fit to fight.

Above: Stephen in Grade Three at Gundagai Primary School. 'This is about the time I knew I would join the Defence Force.' (Stephen Weaver)

Opposite top: Stephen (centre) on his Basic Supplier Course where he received the course Student of Merit award. (Stephen Weaver)

Opposite bottom: Receiving an award from General Allen, Commander of the International Security Assistance Force in 2011. (Stephen Weaver)

I have deployed three times to the Middle East and once to Manus Island in Papua New Guinea. In the former, the desert heat would reach temperatures over 50 degrees and the humidity would be so thick it would hang over the Forward Operating Base like a heavy fog. On one occasion, doing my job to the best of my ability resulted in a commendation, from the Australian Forces Commander, for my leadership in command of up to 400 personnel during a significant attack by the Taliban in 2011.

My current position is with Indigenous Affairs, providing me with an opportunity to extend the reach of Indigenous culture and inculcate it within Air Force culture. My vision is to try to normalise Indigenous culture, particularly through the Senior Leadership Group, to the point that it becomes 'unremarkable' in a way that Welcome to Country and Smoking Ceremonies have become 'Air Force's business as usual.'

Above: Stephen during his Recruit Course in 1987. (Stephen Weaver)
Opposite: Conducting a Physical Training Display at the Tindal Show. (Stephen Weaver)

ALEXANDER TAYLOR

Service Number: 140782
Date of Birth: 10 June 1925
Place of Birth: Charlotte Waters, Northern Territory
Date of Enlistment: 13 July 1943
Place of Enlistment: Adelaide, South Australia
Date of Discharge: 4 March 1946
Rank: Leading Aircraftman
Campaign: Second World War

Alex Taylor was born in the Northern Territory in 1925. At the age of 18, he decided to join the Royal Australian Air Force at No 5 Recruit Centre, Adelaide, South Australia, listing his prior occupation as storeman. He did his recruit training at No 1 Recruit Depot, Shepparton, Victoria, moving on completion to No 1 Aircraft Park, Geelong. In September 1943, he joined No 279 Technical Trainee Course at No 4 School of Technical Training in Adelaide, which he passed, and then moved to No 1 Engineering School in Ascot Vale, Victoria, where he successfully completed No 333 Flight Rigger Course in February 1944. He then proceeded, in March, on posting to No 2 Air Observers School at Mount Gambier, South Australia. Having enlisted as an aircraftman class 1, he reclassified to leading aircraftman on 1 June.

Flight rigging essentially involves the adjustment and travel of moveable flight controls attached to an aircraft's major flying surfaces such as wings and vertical and horizontal stabilisers. Alex's work would have focused on setting cable tensions, adjusting travel limits of flight controls and setting travel stops. In addition to flight controls, he would have also worked on engine and retractable undercarriage components.

On 25 November 1944, Alex posted in to No 4 Personnel Depot, Adelaide, before moving to No 2 Reserve Personnel Pool, Northern Territory, from where he was posted to No 7 Repair and Salvage Unit, Darwin, on 20 December. The role of this unit was to repair damaged aircraft and other equipment, or to salvage spare parts from those beyond repair. Alex remained with this unit for just under ten months, during which the Second World War finally ended.

Above: Mounted on beaching gear, a Catalina is towed for overhaul. (State Library Victoria, Argus Collection)

Opposite: Enlistment photo of Alexander Taylor. (National Archives of Australia)

Alex was then posted to No 20 Squadron, also based in Darwin, on 5 October 1945. At the time, the squadron's Catalinas were heavily involved in repatriating liberated prisoners of war and personnel who had exceeded the allowed time in the tropics. The squadron had formed at Port Moresby, New Guinea, on 1 August 1941 as a General Reconnaissance Flying Boat unit, cooperating, and sharing aircraft and crews, with No 11 Squadron, another flying boat unit based at Port Moresby.

At the outbreak of war in the Pacific, No 20 Squadron's strength was six Catalinas and two Empire flying boats. It performed reconnaissance, anti-submarine patrols, bombing strikes, and the evacuation of civilians away from the Japanese advance.

November 1942 saw No 20 Squadron move to Cairns, Queensland, from where it conducted reconnaissance, anti-submarine patrols and occasional bombing sorties in the waters around New Guinea. In September 1944, the squadron moved to Darwin, as part of No 76 Wing RAAF, their primary purpose being mine laying as far afield as Hong Kong and Wenchow harbours, the furthest north any RAAF aircraft had flown during the war in the Pacific.

In November 1945, No 20 Squadron relocated to RAAF Station Rathmines, New South Wales, disbanding there on 27 March 1946. Alex moved with the squadron to Rathmines but, on 8 February 1946, was posted to No 4 Personnel Depot at Springbank, South Australia, for discharge.

Leading Aircraftman Alexander Taylor discharged from the RAAF on 4 March 1946.

Above: RAAF Station Rathmines became one of the major flying boat bases for the RAAF during the Second World War and housed Nos 9, 11, 20, 40, 41, 43 and 107 Squadrons at various stages during the conflict. (RAAF)

Opposite: Fairey Battles in storage at No 1 Aircraft Depot, Geelong, Victoria. (State Library Victoria, Argus Collection)

ALLAN JOHN WALKER TAYLOR

Service Number: 12133
Date of Birth: 18 May 1910
Place of Birth: Armidale, New South Wales
Date of Enlistment: 21 January 1940
Place of Enlistment: Richmond, New South Wales
Date of Discharge: 7 September 1945
Rank: Sergeant
Campaign: Second World War

Four months short of his 30th birthday, Allan Taylor enlisted in the RAAF, for the duration of the war plus 12 months, at Richmond, New South Wales. He was married to Phyllis Patricia Taylor and had 13 years' experience working as a motor mechanic. Reflecting this experience, Allan enlisted as an Aircraft Hand Mechanic with the rank of aircraftman 1st class.

After the month-long Recruit Drill Course, Allan proceeded to No 3 School of Technical Training in Ultimo, New South Wales, on 20 March 1940, where he joined No 10 Trainee Technical (Fitter) Course with 106 other pupils. Having successfully completed this course, he re-mustered to Fitter IIE and proceeded to No 1 Engineering School in Ascot Vale, Victoria, where he commenced studies on No 55 Fitters IIE course on 12 August 1940.

On 30 November, Allan proceeded on posting to No 1 Air Observers School at Cootamundra, New South Wales, where he was soon reclassified to leading aircraftman. Within months, he was on his way to the United Kingdom, having been selected for service with the Royal Air Force. He proceeded to No 1 Embarkation Depot in Ascot Vale where he underwent kitting, and medical and dental checks, before setting sail on 13 June 1941.

Above: A Lancaster of No 467 Squadron. Sergeant Allan Taylor looks on. (Australian War Memorial).

Opposite: Leuchars, Scotland, circa 1942. Group portrait of ground crew of No 455 Squadron. Allan Taylor is fourth from left. (Australian War Memorial)

Allan arrived in the United Kingdom in August 1941 and was posted to No 102 Squadron, Royal Air Force, which, at the time, was based at Topcliffe in North Yorkshire and operating Whitley Mk.V twin-engine bombers. However, within a few months, the squadron re-equipped with Halifax Mk.II four-engine heavy bombers. As part of Bomber Command, the squadron flew numerous bombing raids over Germany and France. While still with No 102 Squadron, Allan was promoted to temporary corporal.

After eight months serving with No 102 Squadron, Allan was posted to No 455 Squadron on 20 March 1942. Established under Article XV of the Empire Air Training Scheme, the Australian squadron was formed at Swinderby in Lincolnshire on 6 June 1941. At the time Allan joined the squadron, it was based at Wigsley in Nottinghamshire and was operating Hampden twin-engine medium bombers. The squadron was transferred from Bomber Command to Coastal Command in April 1942, after which it operated from several different bases in the United Kingdom as a torpedo bomber unit. On 2 September, Allan was among the support personnel that accompanied 16 of the squadron's aircraft that deployed from Leuchars, Scotland, to Sumburgh, in the Shetland Islands, and from there to northern Russia to protect Allied convoys. In the same month, Allan was promoted to temporary sergeant.

Having returned from Russia by sea as part of an Arctic convoy, Allan was posted to No 467 Squadron, another Article XV unit, in February 1943. The squadron had formed at Scampton, Lincolnshire, in late 1942 and was equipped with Lancaster heavy bombers as part of No 5 Group, Bomber Command. At the time Allan joined the squadron, it was based in Bottesford on the Leicestershire–Lincolnshire county border. In early 1943, the squadron carried out mining operations, known as 'Gardening', off the coast of Bayonne and Saint-Jean-de-Luz, in southern France. The squadron also participated in Bomber Command's campaign over Germany, setting many records within No 5 Group.

Ending his time on operations, Allan was posted from No 467 Squadron to the RAAF's No 11 Personnel Despatch and Receiving Centre at Bournemouth in Sussex ahead of his return to Australia. During his time in the United Kingdom, he had not only served for a period in Russia but also in Canada, Iceland and the United States.

Allan disembarked in Brisbane on 4 December 1944, proceeding to No 2 Personnel Depot at Bradfield Park, New South Wales. On 6 January 1945, he was posted to No 3 Operational Training Unit, a flying boat training unit based at Rathmines. Allan returned to No 2 Personnel Depot where he completed his discharge from the RAAF on 7 September 1945.

Opposite: RAF Bottesford, Leicestershire, England. Sergeant Allan Taylor is fourth from right. (Australian War Memorial)

CHERYL NEAL

Date of Birth: 14 February 1967
Place of Birth: Nowra, New South Wales
Date of Enlistment: 1987
Place of Enlistment: Sydney, New South Wales
Rank: Wing Commander

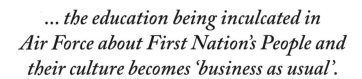

... the education being inculcated in Air Force about First Nation's People and their culture becomes 'business as usual'.

I am a proud Darug (Western Sydney) woman, raised on Yuin (south coast of New South Wales) Country and now living in Ngunnawal Country in the ACT.

After completing primary school in Huskisson on the New South Wales south coast, I went on to Bomaderry High School, finishing up in Year 11 before being offered, and accepting, a job to work for a local vet in Bomaderry.

Coming from a broken home and living independently from my parents, my employer and close friends encouraged me to consider getting out of Nowra and joining the Defence Force to make something of myself. Having grown up in a community with strong ties to the Navy through HMAS *Albatross* meant the idea of Service life wasn't completely foreign to me. This prospect became a reality when I accepted an offer to take up employment with the Air Force as a Medical Assistant.

I joined the Air Force in 1987 and commenced basic training at No 1 Recruit Training Unit in South Australia. While I had mixed feelings about staying in the Air Force after this, the decision to continue would ultimately see me rise through the ranks to be commissioned and enjoy a significant Air Force career.

Opposite: On deployment in Afghanistan in 2012. (Cheryl Neal)

Speaking about those early days, I found the discipline challenging at times and my ability to march was constantly questioned. On the other side, having come from a poor lifestyle, I found that the Mess blew me away – three meals a day and dessert every night, it was like a restaurant and the food was glorious.

After completing initial training, I was posted to No 6 RAAF Hospital in Laverton to train as a medical assistant before my first posting to No 3 RAAF Hospital in Richmond where I would begin applying my skills and learning my trade on the job. A memorable four-year posting to RAAF Base Tindal would follow before recommendations were made for me to look at commissioning.

After completing the necessary studies, I was appointed to a commission, becoming an Air Traffic Controller, that would see me posted to RAAF Base Richmond, working predominately to control and coordinate the RAAF's transport fleet, and then RAAF Base Pearce in Western Australia, where the Australian Defence Force's basic pilot training is conducted. While at Pearce, I met my husband and eventually had twin daughters. With greater demands on my time at home, I opted for a change in employment that would reduce the impact that shift work was having.

That change came in the form of a transfer in category from Air Traffic Control to Administration, which would see me posted from Western Australia to my first posting in Canberra, where postings to the Cadet Branch, Personnel Branch's Career management, No 34 Squadron's Administrative Section, and appointment as Officer Commanding No 1 Alpha Squadron at the Australian Defence Force Academy (one of my favourite postings) followed.

Further postings have included: the RAF's prestigious Staff College in the UK; Joint Operations Command, working on providing personnel support for Australia's operations domestically and overseas; No 28 Squadron, as Commanding Officer; Australian Command and Staff College in Canberra as an Instructor; Deputy Director Diversity and Inclusion Air Force, which would see me actively managing aspects of gender, LGBTQI, Indigenous Affairs, and disabilities; and then finally Defence Force Recruiting where I finally made the decision to transfer to the RAAF Reserves.

However, having just retired from the permanent Air Force, I was invited to return to take up the position as Senior Indigenous Liaison Officer working for Air Commander Australia.

Opposite top: Cheryl during NAIDOC week in Canberra, 2017. (RAAF)

Opposite bottom: Indigenous Liaison Team members at the Australian War Memorial celebrating the Air Force's Centenary in 2021. (RAAF)

Given my background and the enthusiasm in this area, this posting was quite fitting and I quickly set about supporting and promoting the newly established Indigenous Liaison Officer positions, with First Nations People taking up these posts. Among my aspirations is to ensure the education being inculcated in Air Force about First Nations People and our culture becomes 'business as usual', rather than something thought about only during NAIDOC week.

When I think about the Air Force for Aboriginal and Torres Strait Islanders, I think about opportunities; also, I have taken to the saying, 'I'm not a product of my circumstances, I'm a product of my decisions'. However, the quote that you might be surprised that is my favourite, when I look back at where I came from, is our Air Force's motto, 'Per Ardua Ad Astra' (through struggle to the stars).

I continue to enjoy my employment with the Air Force and am looking forward to returning to the Reserves later in 2022.

> *... the Mess blew me away – three meals a day – and dessert every night, it was like a restaurant and the food was glorious.*

Opposite top: Cheryl's great-great-grandmother, Darug woman Jenny Swift (nee Lock), is bottom left. (Cheryl Neal)

Opposite bottom: Cheryl graduating from officer training in 1992. (Cheryl Neal)

Russell & Sons
17, BAKER STREET W.A
40, BRECKNOCK ROAD N.
PHOTOGRAPHERS TO H.M. THE QUEEN.

NORMA LILLIAN FEDER

Service Number: 111614
Date of Birth: 4 August 1925
Place of Birth: Moonta Mines, South Australia
Date of Enlistment: 30 November 1943
Place of Enlistment: Adelaide, South Australia
Date of Discharge: 25 February 1946
Rank: Aircraftwoman
Campaign: Second World War

Norma Feder, a Narungga/Narangga woman, was born in Moonta Mines at the top of the Yorke Peninsula in South Australia in 1925. Aged 18 and still living at home with her parents in November 1943, she presented to No 5 Recruiting Centre. Carrying a consent form signed by her mother, Alice Evelyn Feder, Norma applied to join the Women's Auxiliary Australian Air Force (WAAAF). In the same month, the centre had processed applications from 354 aspiring aircrew, 432 ground staff and 88 WAAAFs.

In her enlistment application, Norma noted her civilian occupation as 'home duties' and her preferred mustering as Stewardess. However, after undergoing the enlistment formalities, she enlisted as a Cook's Assistant for the duration of the war plus 12 months. Her rank was aircraftwoman 1. Although aged just 18, she was authorised to draw an adult rate of pay.

Norma underwent recruit training at No 4 Initial Training School (4ITS) at Mount Breckan, Victor Harbour, South Australia. The school, centred around a grand mansion that remains a landmark in the town, had initially formed on 4 November 1940 to train aircrew. Its WAAAF Training Centre commenced to function on 8 March 1942. Between those dates and when 4ITS disbanded on 3 December 1944, it graduated 5,595 aircrew and 2,604 WAAAFs.

Above: WAAAF training. (Mitchell Library, State Library of New South Wales)

Opposite: Enlistment photo of Norma Feder. (National Archives of Australia)

At 4ITS, Norma joined 61 other WAAAF recruits on No R71 Recruit Drill Course, passing out on 31 December 1943. The two preceding courses, from which 70 additional WAAAFs graduated, had completed earlier in the month. After graduation, Norma was posted to 4ITS on staff, effective from 5 January 1944. While initially reported as under training, she must have impressed because, on 7 August 1944, the school's Commanding Officer recommended her as suitable for promotion or reclassification. The recommendation was made as Norma departed 4ITS to undertake training as a Cook at No 4 School of Technical Training.

Formed on 1 April 1940 at Headquarters Southern Area in Adelaide, South Australia, the school moved shortly thereafter to the Exhibition Buildings on Adelaide's North Terrace. The school provided courses for riggers, service police, welders, storekeepers, trainee technicians, cooks, mess stewards, recruit drill, fitter armourers, and dental orderlies and technicians. Although initially students were accommodated in tents on the Exhibition Buildings' oval, subsequently the Dunlop Building and St Mark's College, on Pennington Terrace in North Adelaide, were taken over to provide accommodation for airmen and WAAAFs respectively. Training ceased at the unit on 5 October 1945, by which time 21,913 trainees had passed through the school.

In August 1944, when Norma arrived at the school, there were 1,349 pupils under training. The intake of pupils for August alone was 543. Norma joined No 242 Cooks Course which she successfully completed on 23 November. As a result, she was re-mustered to Cook on the following day.

Norma was next posted on staff to No 4 Personnel Depot at Springbank, starting there on 4 December. The depot had first formed at St Mark's College as No 4 Embarkation Depot on 25 November 1940. Its initial role was the final preparation of South Australian aircrew trainees for embarkation. However, in April 1944, the depot was renamed No 4 Personnel Depot as its role broadened to encompass the return and eventual demobilisation of RAAF personnel following the end of hostilities. By the end of September 1946, when it proceeded to disband, the depot had managed the discharge of 19,613 RAAF personnel.

On 11 February 1946, Norma was also posted to No 4 Personnel Depot for discharge, becoming one of 219 WAAAF and 1,558 RAAF members who discharged from the depot that month.

Aircraftwoman Norma Feder discharged from No 4 Personnel Depot on 25 February.

Opposite: Meal time. (Mitchell Library, State Library of New South Wales)

DAVID VALENTINE PAUL DFC

Service Number: 403215
Date of Birth: 10 June 1920
Place of Birth: North Sydney, New South Wales
Date of Enlistment: 4 January 1941
Place of Enlistment: Sydney, New South Wales
Date of Discharge: 29 October 1945
Rank: Squadron Leader
Campaign: Second World War

David Paul was born in mid-1920. Born and raised in North Sydney, David was the great-grandson of Lucy Frazer, a Ngoorabul woman from the Severn River region of New South Wales, but he kept his heritage quiet. After leaving school, he worked as a labourer, on Queensland and New South Wales properties, and as a dry cleaner.

In 1939, he applied to enlist in the RAAF but was rejected. Not discouraged, he enrolled in night school where he worked hard and, after applying again, was accepted to train as a pilot on 4 January 1941 on enlistment in Sydney.

In the interest of truthful reporting it has to be admitted that the loss of Horsley and Paul has shaken the Squadron far more than the loss of any other crews during November.

No 454 Squadron operations record book entry, 4 December 1943

Opposite: Studio portrait of Flight Lieutenant David Valentine Paul DFC. (Australian War Memorial)

In April of the same year, he was sent to Rhodesia (now Zimbabwe), where he trained in the Empire Air Training Scheme, and was awarded his wings in December. David was a keen and dedicated pupil and was posted as a pilot to No 454 Squadron in North Africa where he flew Baltimore bombers on 95 sorties over the Aegean Sea.

Planned as one of the 17 Australian-manned squadrons for the Royal Air Force (RAF), No 454 Squadron was formed on 23 May 1941 and disbanded on 11 July 1941, at Williamtown, New South Wales. Finally, with RAAF technical personnel already in the Middle East and newly arrived RAF ground crew, it reformed on 30 September 1942 at Aqir, Palestine, as a light bomber squadron. At Quiarra, the first of the Blenheim V refresher courses began, but, in February 1943, No 454 Squadron was moved westward to LG.91 (Amiriya South), about 45 miles from Alexandria, Egypt. It was attached to No 201 Group, RAF Middle East. The squadron quickly converted to the Baltimore Mk.III, an American-built light bomber. The unit was required to provide armed convoy escorts and independent anti-submarine patrols for the many Allied troop and supply convoys from Egypt, and fuel tankers from the Levant oil terminals, destined for Malta and other Eighth Army forward bases. Anti-submarine patrols during daylight hours were increasingly augmented by independent armed visual reconnaissances and shipping strikes over the Aegean Sea. There were strong Axis garrisons and formidable air units to contend with in the outer defended ring (Athens–Rhodes–Crete–southern Greece and the Dodecanese Islands).

On 4 December 1943, during a bombing operation, David was shot down by a Messerschmitt Bf 109. During this sortie, he showed outstanding courage and skill. The attack by the fighter caused significant damage and, with his aircraft burning fiercely, David made a perfect landing on the sea. The burning fuel from the aircraft spread out over the water and the crew were forced to swim underwater to escape. One of them was unable to swim the distance due to injury. David, although suffering severe burns to his hands, swam back through the flames and brought the injured man to safety. This was David's 95th operational sortie; he had been due to go on leave a few days later. Instead, he and his crew were rescued by the Germans and taken prisoner, spending the rest of the war as prisoners of war in Stalag IV-B, Mühlberg. This camp was one of the largest in Germany and housed many British and Australian servicemen after the fall of Greece. It was liberated by Soviet soldiers on 23 April 1945. At the time of liberation, there were nearly 30,000 prisoners crammed into the camp.

Although a commissioned officer in a non-ranking prisoner of war camp, David was held in very high regard by fellow prisoners of all nations. His unflagging cheerfulness, courage and compassion were an example to all.

Above: Formal portrait of RAN and RAAF officers at the Australian Joint Anti-Submarine School at HMAS *Albatross* at Nowra, New South Wales. The only identified officer is Flight Lieutenant David Valentine Paul DFC RAAF at front row far left. (Australian War Memorial)

Opposite: Prisoners of war line the side of the road as an Anzac Day march proceeds at a German prisoner of war camp. Identified leading the march is Flight Officer David Valentine Paul DFC, No 454 Squadron. (Australian War Memorial)

While a prisoner of war, David was awarded the Distinguished Flying Cross. The award was gazetted on 28 March 1944.

> Pilot Officer Paul has taken part in many varied types of operational sorties; including anti-submarine patrols, long-range reconnaissance and bombing sorties. These sorties were flown in the face of considerable enemy opposition and on 9 occasions, he flew his aircraft, through anti-aircraft fire, at low altitude to obtain photographs of enemy invasion barges and supply ships. Enemy aircraft were often encountered and Pilot Officer Paul was chased, unsuccessfully by 3 hostile fighters. He has, at all times, displayed outstanding leadership, initiative and determination.

After the war, he went on to serve in the RAAF Reserve after reaching the rank of squadron leader. He then returned to Sydney where he began a distinguished career in the New South Wales Police Force, working as a detective in high profile criminal investigation cases. He died on 14 May 1973, aged 52, at RAAF Base Richmond.

Opposite: No 454 Squadron operations record book showing the entry recording the loss of Horsley and Paul. (National Archives of Australia)

			Summary of Events	References to Appendices
Place	Date	Time		

	Dec 3rd.	Three other crews carried out Aegean trips, but again the area was quiet, although W/O McCRABB saw a ship of one thousand tons in PARTENI BAY, LEROS, and two F-boats entering KOS HARBOUR.

During the afternoon F/O CAREW searched the route up to ANTI-KYTHERA in case HORSLEY had ditched, but saw nothing.

133089 F/O OVENSTONE, D, returned from No. 3 M.E.T.S. on completing an aircraft recognition course.

| | Dec 4th. | And now Dave Paul is missing. Like HORSLEY's, one of the squadron's original and steadiest crews. He took off at 0625 and sent a sighting at 0928. Later other aircraft intercepted a signal "Closing W/T watch owing to probable attack from enemy aircraft". The crew are :- |

A. 405215 W/O PAUL D.V. - PILOT.	A.400954 W/O AGG G.T. - NAVIGATOR.	
A. 406684 W/O SIMPSON R.M. WOP/AG.	645357 W/O RENNIE J. - WOP/AG.	

It was PAUL's last trip before completion of his tour, and RENNIE had an extension and was well over the total number of hours required to complete his tour.

In the interest of truthful reporting, it has to be admitted that the loss of HORSLEY and PAUL has shaken the squadron far more than the loss of any other crews during November.

This may be because HORSLEY and PAUL have gone on succeeding days, but it is more likely because they were both old and experienced crews. When crews such as JOINER's and CLARKSON's went, older members of the squadron reassured themselves by reflecting that CLARKSON and JOINER were comparatively inexperienced. Now that HORSLEY and PAUL have failed to return, that comfort is denied them.

The other three recce aircraft made no sightings worth having, W/O LLOYD's or E-boats, both at PAROS and in the STENNO PASS, being the best. W/O LLOYD's trip brought him to five hundred hours and he becomes the first member of the squadron to finish a tour. Fittingly he was invited to the Officer's Mess, after the talk, and plied with liquor.

N.Z.405448 F/SGT LAWSON is to-day promoted to Temporary Warrant Officer.

| | Dec 5th. | After the excitement of the last two days everything is tranquil again. Four Aegean sorties were largely unproductive. A one thousand ton ship in SYROS and many caiques, seen by F/O PARKIN, alone meriting mention. |

F/SGT MITCHELL did a training anti-submarine patrol.

YASMIN WATSON

Date of Birth: 10 October 1992
Place of Birth: Melbourne, Victoria
Date of Enlistment: 4 October 2011
Rank: Corporal

> *I also received full flight-line qualification which allowed me to carry out jobs outside of my role, such as refuelling and multiple other servicings, enabling me to fly with the C-17 anywhere in the world.*

I am a Kamilaroi woman, the second largest mob in Australia. Unfortunately, my Pop, who was half-Aboriginal and a part of the stolen generation, passed away when I was five years old. There is a knowledge gap as a result. At the moment, my younger sister is on a full scholarship with the Yalari program at Kinross Wolaroi in Orange. She is currently learning a lot.

Enlisting in October 2011, I commenced recruit training at No 1 Recruit Training Unit (1RTU) and was soon back-coursed due to failing the fitness test. Eventually becoming super fit, I was ready to go back on course and was given an opportunity to go to Singleton and carry out the role of sentry guard while Defence personnel carried out the detonation of explosives. While I was carrying out a long-distance run, I started to experience numbness in both of my feet and was taken straight to medical; eventually, after multiple scans, MRI and pressure testing, I was diagnosed with anterior compartment syndrome. In April 2012, I had surgery on both legs. The CO of 1RTU was kind enough to delay my medical discharge and, within a month of the surgery, I was deemed fully fit and placed on the next recruit course on 19 June 2012.

Opposite: Commander Andrew Watson with his daughter, Corporal Yasmin Watson, at HMAS Albatross Nowra. (RAAF)

I graduated on 29 August. This was after a very challenging time; it was a huge accomplishment and a day I will never forget. I also received an award called the 'Yasmin Watson PT Excellence Award'! I was then posted to the RAAF School of Technical Training but, due to my initial back course, missed the Initial Employment Training (IET) course. As luck would have it, there was a contract changeover and I was informed I would have to wait at least a year for the next Life Support IET course. I was then offered a General Hand role back at 1RTU, where I assisted the logistics section. While I was there, I had opportunities to mentor the recruits coming through the rehab section, proudly represented the women's RAAF soccer team in 2012, assisted the Airfield Defence Guard instructors with enemy parties and gained a lot of knowledge and experience from the sergeant, corporal and leading aircraftwoman equipment personnel.

I eventually commenced IET in September 2013 and graduated in May 2014. As an Aeronautical Life Support Fitter, my role involves servicing/maintaining all safety and survival equipment – such as life rafts, helmets, oxygen masks, life preservers, and survival jackets – across the Australian Defence Force (ADF). It also involves fitting the majority of these items to aircrew across all manned aviation platforms in the ADF including helicopters, trainers, fighter jets and transport aircraft.

Opposite: Corporal Yasmin Watson inside an Air Force C-17 Globemaster. (RAAF)

I was then posted to No 36 Squadron on the C-17 Globemaster for four years. I had the opportunity to represent the squadron at the 2015 Avalon Airshow. I also received full flight-line qualification which allowed me to carry out jobs outside of my role, such as refuelling and multiple other servicings, enabling me to fly with the C-17 anywhere in the world. I had the amazing opportunities of travelling to Hawaii, San Antonio (where we delivered a C-17 for its deep-level maintenance in 2016 and again in 2018), El Paso, Diego Garcia, and the Middle East in 2016 and 2018 (Al Minhad, Abu Dhabi, Baghdad, Kabul, Al-Taqaddium and Al Asad). All were absolutely wonderful experiences I will never forget.

Once my four years with No 36 Squadron were up, I was then posted to HMAS *Albatross* and 808 Squadron. This was a fantastic opportunity to work with, and learn about, a different Service. It was also a great opportunity and challenge to learn to train Sailors to fit and repair life-support equipment on land and at sea, while also carrying out scheduled maintenance, repairs and fitment of jackets, helmets and cold-weather suits. It was truly a fantastic and challenging three years, from 2019–2021, supporting the MRH90 helicopter through the 2019 bushfires, floods, *Fiji Assist* and Covid-19. I can't emphasise enough how much knowledge and experience I gained during those three years. At the beginning of 2022, I was posted to 725 Squadron, the training unit for Seahawk Romeo helicopters, on promotion. I can't wait to continue the journey with the Navy.

On top of all of my achievements working with No 36 Squadron and now the Navy, it's always a proud moment marching with my father on Anzac Day in my home of Nowra.

Not having had the smoothest run career-wise in the RAAF, and facing challenges and a lot of speed humps in the ten years I've been in, I believe failing shouldn't have the negative stigma that it carries; we gain so much by failing. I believe we should 'Fail early, fail often, but always fail forward.'

GLENARD RONALD WEETRA

Service Number: 141512
Date of Birth: 22 September 1925
Place of Birth: Adelaide, South Australia
Date of Enlistment: 9 November 1943
Place of Enlistment: Adelaide, South Australia
Date of Discharge: 11 March 1946.
Rank: Leading Aircraftman
Campaign: Second World War

Glenard was born on 22 September 1925 in Adelaide, South Australia. Leaving his job as a garage assistant, he joined the Royal Australian Air Force at No 5 Recruiting Centre in Adelaide at the age of 18 as an Aircraft Hand.

After training at No 1 Recruit Depot, Shepparton, he was posted as an aircraftman 1 to No 6 Service Flying Training School at Mallala, South Australia. He was then posted to Townsville, Queensland, and No 1 Reserve Personnel Pool while awaiting his transfer to No 5 Communication Unit which took place on 9 June 1944. While at the latter, he was promoted to leading aircraftman.

Communication units were flight-size units that flew various aircraft types for communications between RAAF units and as VIP transports. The previously named No 5 Communication Flight was formed at Garbutt Airfield in Townsville in December 1942 and provided communications for the North-Eastern Area.

Glenard was posted to No 82 Squadron in late 1944, embarking for the Dutch East Indies. The squadron was initially equipped with Kittyhawk and Airacobra fighters and formed at Bankstown, New South Wales, in June 1943. In May 1944, it relocated to Ross River airfield near Townsville and, soon after its arrival, the squadron flew its first combat sorties, bombing and strafing targets at Sorong. Ground attack operations, as well as barge sweeps along the New Guinea coast, became the focus of the squadron's efforts for the next six months. In 1945, it moved to Morotai from where it flew convoy patrols around Borneo and assisted ground forces in operations against bypassed Japanese garrisons.

Above: New RAAF recruits marching off parade. (State Library Victoria, Argus Collection)

Opposite: Enlistment photo of Glenard Weetra. (National Archives of Australia)

June 1945 saw the squadron operating from Labuan Island while providing close air support to Australian troops during operations on Borneo. The most successful strike during this period occurred in mid-August when several Kittyhawks caught Japanese aircraft about to take off from Kuching airfield. Four enemy aircraft were destroyed, and two others damaged, before the fighters turned their attention to barge traffic on the Sarawak River. Almost as soon as hostilities ceased, No 82 Squadron was informed it would form part of the British Commonwealth Occupation Force that was to garrison a defeated Japan. The unit converted to Mustangs and, in March 1946, moved to Bofu in Japan. It was engaged on surveillance patrols over Japan until it disbanded at Iwakuni on 22 October 1948.

Glenard served with No 82 Squadron for over a year before being posted to No 38 Operational Base Unit on 17 October 1945. The unit was based on Morotai, Balikpapan. Operational base units were set up as a network to provide emergency and designated landing grounds to support the safe transit of aircraft across Australia and into the South-West Pacific and, in some cases if required, to effect repairs and servicing of aircraft in transit. Some were on major bases, but most were set up to cover transit routes between major fixed bases and operational areas. They were of particular value during the repatriation of former prisoners of war and tour-expired personnel, and for traffic headed the other way as Japan was 'occupied' post-war.

Finishing his tour of duty in late 1945, Glenard returned to Australia on 30 November and a posting to No 4 Personnel Depot followed as he awaited discharge.

Glenard Weetra was discharged from the RAAF on 11 March 1946.

Opposite top: A jeep trailer, presented to the YMCA by the Shepparton High School Old Boys Association, seen in operation on the RAAF airstrip at Morotai. (State Library Victoria, Argus Collection)

Opposite bottom: RAAF Station Malalla, South Australia. (RAAF)

JODI ROSS

Date of Birth: 4 May 1971
Place of Birth: Sydney, New South Wales
Date of Enlistment: 13 April 1989
Rank: Warrant Officer

> *Getting to know the Chiefs and their families has been a real honour ...*

I am a proud Wiradjuri woman, however grew up on Ngunnawal/Ngambri Country. I joined the Air Force when I was 17 years old. I am very proud that my daughter also followed in my footsteps and is a member of the Air Force, Leading Aircraftwoman Georgia Ross.

I originally signed up as a Steward, but went on to become a Cook and, finally, a Personnel Capability Specialist in 1999. I have held many postings around the country, including at RAAF Williams and RAAF Richmond. I was also the Valet to two Chiefs of the Air Force, of which I have many amazing memories.

Over my 33 years of service, I have had so many experiences and opportunities. I have formed amazing friendships, especially from when I was in catering; we were, and still are, like a family. While I haven't been in catering for over 20 years, some of those people are still my closet friends.

Working personally for two Chiefs was a real honour and privilege. I can still remember the day I was having my interview with the Chief (Air Marshal Geoffrey Shepherd AO), I came downstairs with my long sleeve shirt and tie on. My husband said 'Jodi, are you for real wearing that shirt? It has train tracks on the sleeve' (part of the job of a Valet is looking after the Chief's uniforms); he then re-ironed the shirt. I got the job. Getting to

Opposite: Operation *Mazurka* in the Sinai, Egypt, 2011. (RAAF)

know the Chiefs and their families has been a real honour; I was able to see and interact with them in their home life. I became very close to Air Marshal Shepherd's family, so much so that I got invited to their son's wedding and I still go and stay with the family to this day.

On one occasion I attended the 70th birthday of RAAF Butterworth in Malaysia, stayed at the same hotel as the Chief and was treated like a VIP. It was incredible.

> *Looking back, I pinch myself as I would still think of myself as a dumb-arse kid that did not finish school! I cannot believe the opportunities I have been given.*

Above: Jodi conducting community engagement at Batchelor in the Northern Territory during Exercise *Pitch Black 2018*. (RAAF)

Opposite: Exercise *Kummundoo 2019* in Broome, Western Australia. This exercise was run in conjunction with National Aboriginal Community Controlled Health Organisation, delivering dental services to remote communities. (RAAF)

EDGAR SAMUEL LOCKYER

Service Number: A5439
Date of Birth: 21 April 1914
Place of Birth: Roebourne, Western Australia
Date of Enlistment: 27 July 1947
Place of Enlistment: Pearce, Western Australia
Date of Discharge: 14 April 1955
Rank: Corporal
Campaign: Malayan Emergency

Edgar 'Eddie' Lockyer was born 21 April 1914 at Mullina Station, Roebourne, Western Australia. He enlisted in the Citizen Air Force, the active reserve component of the Royal Australian Air Force, on 21 July 1947 at RAAF Pearce. Prior to enlistment, Edgar was working as a temporary technician with the Postmaster-General's Department. Before that he had worked as a technician transmission and long line communications, and as a garage mechanic. He was married to Kathleen Lockyer and had five children to support with an additional two more being born while in service.

In 1943, before joining the RAAF, Edgar completed the Radio Service Engineering Course offered by the Australian Radio College Pty Ltd. At his pre-enlistment trade test conducted on 2 July 1947, Edgar was found to have aptitude for radio and was offered enlistment as a Trainee Group IV (Wireless Maintenance Mechanic Category 1). After enlistment, Edgar undertook No 12 Recruit Drill Course at Pearce between 11 August and 19 September 1947. He was then posted to the Air and Ground Radio School in Ballarat, Victoria, where he successfully undertook No 1 Course Radio Servicemen 'Ground' Serial 2. It was a 22-week-long course that commenced on 2 October. Notably, Edgar's end of course assessment was 'Proficient with distinction'. Not surprisingly, on 12 November, Edgar was specially recommended for the radio trade in the Permanent Air Force and, on 25 March 1948, the day the course concluded, he re-mustered as a Radio Serviceman Group 3. He then remained on staff at the school employed on installation duties where, on 26 June 1948, he reclassified as a leading aircraftman.

On 21 July 1948, Edgar was posted to No 1 Aircraft Depot, located at RAAF Station Laverton, Victoria. However, he very soon applied for a compassionate posting to No 3 Telecommunication Unit, situated about ten kilometres from RAAF Station Pearce, so he could re-join his growing family. He was granted this posting with effect from 13 September 1948. The unit, long regarded as the home of the RAAF Signals Operators trade, had formed in October 1946 and performed specialist communications tasks providing strategic and tactical support to the Australian Defence Force, both in Australia and overseas, for the next 45 years.

Edgar discharged from the Citizen Air Force on 6 October 1948 so he could enlist in the Permanent Air Force the next day, which he did for a period of 12 years. This process resulted in his re-muster to Wireless Maintenance Mechanic Group 1 and reclassification to aircraftman class 1 on 21 February 1949. It would be another year before he was again reclassified to leading aircraftman.

Opposite: Enlistment photo of Edgar. (National Archives of Australia)

Between March and November 1951, while on posted strength with No 90 Wing, Edgar deployed with unit personnel to Labuan Island, off north-west Borneo, for duty with the Royal Air Force (RAF) detachment based there. When the Australian contingent arrived in Labuan, they were greeted by the entire RAF detachment comprising 23 men and two dogs. The wing operated during the early years of the Malayan Emergency and had administrative control of No 1 (Bomber) Squadron, operating Avro Lincolns, and No 38 (Transport) Squadron (Douglas C-47 Dakotas). The Lincolns generally conducted area bombing missions as well as precision strikes to harass communist insurgents, while the Dakotas were tasked with air lifting cargo, VIPs, troops and casualties, as well as courier and supply drops.

Working and living conditions at Labuan were challenging, limited to tents and earthen floors; persistent tropical downpours led to flooding and the ground inside being waterlogged. Equally challenging was the work at the end of the runway, where Edgar and his colleagues would often find themselves submitting to long and tedious shifts in less than adequate radio shacks.

During the Second World War, Edgar's brother, Flight Sergeant Arnold Lockyer, had been killed by the Japanese while a prisoner of war and was buried in the Labuan War Cemetery. Knowing this, on Anzac Day 1951, Edgar's Officer in Charge marched a body of men to the gates of the cemetery where they formed two ranks and, as a mark of respect, gave Edgar the honour of laying a wreath under the flagpole.

At the time, policy dictated that tours for ground staff to No 90 Wing would be of nine to twelve months duration. Accordingly, Edgar posted back to No 3 Telecommunication Unit on 14 November 1951, where, in December, he was provisionally promoted to corporal. Provisional promotions were made ahead of airmen passing the relevant trade test and, where appropriate, promotion examination. However, feeling civilian employment offered more opportunities for him to look after his burgeoning family, Edgar applied for early discharge. His request was granted and, on 14 March 1955, Edgar posted into Base Squadron Pearce ahead of discharge.

Corporal Edgar S. Lockyer discharged from the Royal Australian Air Force at his own request at RAAF Pearce on 16 March 1955 after serving for eight years.

Edgar's memorial, at the Lockyer Brothers Memorial in Western Australia. (State Library of Western Australia)

VALMA JUNE WEETRA

Service Number: 114670
Date of Birth: 7 June 1924
Place of Birth: Adelaide, South Australia
Date of Enlistment: 13 December 1944
Place of Enlistment: Adelaide, South Australia
Date of Discharge: 3 December 1946
Rank: Aircraftwoman
Campaign: Second World War

Valma Weetra was born in mid-1924 in Adelaide, South Australia. At the age of 20, she decided to join the Women's Auxiliary Australian Air Force (WAAAF) and enlisted at No 5 Recruit Centre in her hometown. Interestingly, she listed her previous occupation as a 'messenger' on arrival into the WAAAF, but she was employed as a Cook's Assistant.

Valma conducted her training at No 1 WAAAF Depot, completing No 268 Recruits Course in January 1945 before being posted to Central Gunnery School (CGS) at Cressy, Victoria. At the time of her posting, Valma was one of 39 WAAAF personnel posted to the school.

Above: Ex-servicewomen marching, March 1954. (John Oxley Library, State Library of Queensland)
Opposite: Enlistment photo of Valma Weetra. (National Archives of Australia)

Raised on 5 June 1942 at Sale, Victoria, under the command of No 1 Training Group, the CGS received its first aircraft, three Beauforts, on 7 July 1942, just prior to the school moving to Williamtown, New South Wales, on 10 July. On 19 July, five officers and five airmen Wireless Operator/Air Gunners arrived for No 1 Gunnery Leaders Course. In November 1942, CGS moved to Mildura, Victoria. The strength of the unit at this time was recorded as eight officers and 104 airmen.

The school made its final move on 23 June 1943 to RAAF Base Cressy, which had been established as a site for training and operational unit personnel to improve their readiness for operational flying and was the home of the Armament Training Station from July 1939 until April 1942. At the time of the move, the strength of the unit consisted of 17 officers, 101 airmen and three WAAAFs. CGS gradually ran down its training and, in January 1946, it was renamed Care and Maintenance Unit before being disbanded on 19 July.

Aircraftwoman Valma Weetra spent all her time at the school before discharging on 3 December 1946. As one of around 27,000 women who served in the WAAAF, Valma would have been employed in a trade that had previously been performed by men. At the peak of the war in July 1944, WAAAF personnel filled musterings such as accounting machine operators, flight mechanics, flight riggers, mess stewards, meterological assistants, wireless mechanics, and wireless telegraphists, to name a few.

Valma discharged from the WAAAF at Laverton on 3 December 1946.

Above: Cressy Airfield, Victoria. (RAAF)

JAMES TERRANCE SINCLAIR

Service Number: 412085
Date of Birth: 15 February 1912
Place of Birth: Bangalow, New South Wales
Date of Enlistment: 21 June 1941
Place of Enlistment: Sydney, New South Wales
Date of Discharge: 14 May 1948
Rank: Flight Lieutenant
Campaign: Second World War

James Sinclair was born in 1912 at Bangalow, New South Wales. He was the grandson of an Aboriginal Boer War veteran from the South Coast, Kangaroo Valley mob so is possibly a descendant of Yuin Nation.

At the age of 29, James enlisted in the Royal Australian Air Force at No 2 Recruiting Centre on 21 June 1941. Prior to his enlistment, he held jobs as a cabinet maker, wireless mechanic, storeman and foreman. On enlistment, he named his mother, Nora Jean Green, as his next of kin.

James was awarded his Flying Badge on 8 January 1942 after completion of training at No 3 Service Flying Training School and granted a commission in April 1944. Later that year, he was promoted to flying officer. After additional training on several different aircraft types, he was posted to No 24 Squadron to fly B-24 Liberators.

He first saw active service on Morotai, a small island in the Netherlands East Indies, having embarked from Darwin in June 1945. The Allies used this island during the Second World War as a base to support the liberation of the Philippines.

Opposite: Donning parachutes at No 3 Service Flying Training School, Amberley. (State Library Victoria, Argus Collection)

In July, James took part in the Battle of Balikpapan, which saw Allied forces conduct a large-scale amphibious landing supported by air and naval forces. A port on the southern coast of Dutch Borneo, Balikpapan was the site of the last major Australian ground operation of the Second World War. The landing was code-named *Oboe Two* and was the largest of the *Oboe* operations mounted by I Corps at various places around Borneo. The landing's objectives were to secure oil processing and port facilities. After a tremendous preparatory bombardment, the 7th Division went ashore on the morning of 1 July 1945. It was the first time during the war the division was deployed in its entirety all at once. Once ashore, the division had to fight much harder for its beachhead than the forces at the earlier *Oboe* landings at Tarakan or Brunei Bay; concerted Japanese resistance continued for the next three weeks as the Australians advanced inland. The operational tempo decreased thereafter but daily engagements with the Japanese continued until the war's end.

Balikpapan was one of the most controversial Australian operations of the Second World War. By this point, it was clear Australian operations in Borneo were not contributing anything to the final defeat of Japan and many high-ranking Australian officers considered them strategically unsound. The Australian Commander-in-Chief, General Sir Thomas Blamey, advised the government to withdraw its support for *Oboe Two*. The government, however, stood behind the Commander-in-Chief of the South-West Pacific Area, General Douglas MacArthur, who had devised the *Oboe* operations, and the Balikpapan landings went ahead. They resulted in the deaths of 229 Australians and around 1,800 Japanese.

James returned to Australia in December 1945 where he served at Tocumwal Airfield on the New South Wales/Victorian border. This base was originally established by the United States Army Air Force and named McIntyre Field. The RAAF took over operation of the airfield and renamed it RAAF Station Tocumwal. Up to 4,500 RAAF personnel, and 400 WAAAFs, were based there. Tocumwal was also home for up to 54 Liberators, 11 Vultee Vengeances, five Kittyhawks and an Airspeed Oxford. It was also a vast storage and repair depot for a wide range of RAAF aircraft.

James continued his service after the war and was promoted to temporary flight lieutenant in February 1946. On 6 March, while attached to No 46 Care and Maintenance Unit, he was delivering a Mosquito to Amberley, Queensland, for storage when it crashed on take-off, injuring him and his passenger.

Flight Lieutenant James Sinclair discharged from the Royal Australian Air Force on 14 May 1948.

Above: No 24 Squadron Liberator crew walk to their aircraft before an operation. (State Library Victoria, Argus Collection)

Opposite: Enlistment photo of James Sinclair. (National Archives of Australia)

MICHAEL ENCHONG

Date of Birth:	31 July 1964
Place of Birth:	Wagga Wagga, New South Wales
Place of Enlistment:	Townsville, Queensland
Date of Enlistment:	1986
Date of Discharge:	2020
Rank:	Warrant Officer

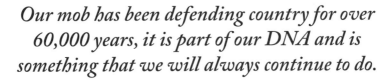

Our mob has been defending country for over 60,000 years, it is part of our DNA and is something that we will always continue to do.

Michael Enchong's father was a proud Torres Strait Islander man from the Darnley and Mer Islands, while his mother was of Maori heritage from the Ngati Whatua community, located in the North Island of New Zealand.

While Michael was born in Wagga Wagga on Wiradjuri Country, he mainly grew up in Bowen on Juru Country in North Queensland, playing rugby league and cricket and then making the most of Bowen's local fishing, catching the likes of mud and sand crabs, squid, mussels, oysters and fish, and occasionally taking a feed of turtle.

Michael's father was the first in his family to serve, joining the Merchant Navy during the Second World War and providing material support to the war effort as a 14-year-old. He would go on to join the Army, seeing action in Korea and then in the Malayan Emergency.

Growing up, Michael would eventually complete an apprenticeship as an electrical fitter mechanic and applied for various jobs, including those in the mines and nickel plants. However, it would not be until he saw a Defence Force recruiting advertisement for Electricians – that guaranteed further trade skills training, job and financial security for his family, and an opportunity to see much of the country – that he would make the decision to join the Air Force in 1986.

Opposite: Warrant Officer Michael Enchong. (Michael Enchong) Above: Warrant Officer Michael Enchong Australian War Memorial. (Michael Enchong)

216

> *... collectively our family now has over 100 years of service in various elements of the ADF.*

After five years as a qualified Air Force Facilities Electrician, Michael changed trades, becoming a Communication Electronic Technician (CETECH) and moving on to a posting at RAAF Base Pearce in Western Australia. As a CETECH, Michael worked on a number of communication systems including Air Traffic Control Communications, the Precision Approach Radar, and High Frequency Air Operations Communications Centres; he also did a stint in an instructional role for the then Communications Systems Controller Course.

During his career, Michael served at various bases around Australia including Sydney, Melbourne, Perth, Townsville, Brisbane and Canberra, and deployed to Malaysia and the Cocos Islands.

A switch in employment saw Michael working in Air Force's Personnel Branch and becoming responsible for conducting numerous First Nations Youth Programs at a number of bases, helping to give First Nations youth a snapshot of what life and jobs would look like as an Aviator, in an attempt to break down barriers and misconceptions that would often prevent them from seeing employment and careers in the Air Force as achievable. 'Proudly, we were able to deploy Health capabilities to three locations and highlight to our communities some of the roles that Air Force deploys whilst delivering positive health outcomes to the local communities.'

In the course of Michael's career, he proudly saw many of his own family take up employment with the ADF. His brother John joined the Army as an infantryman before transferring to the Medical Corps to work as an Inspector Health, Preventive Medicine, deploying to Rwanda in that capacity; he retired with 20 years of service.

Michael's children also joined the ADF: John as a Maritime Warfare Officer with the Royal Australian Navy, Jason with the Royal Australian Armoured Corps, and Tara as an Intelligence Analyst with the Royal Australian Air Force.

While Michael is very proud of following in his father's footsteps in joining the ADF, he and his wife are particularly proud their children have independently followed his own path to join the ADF 'where their growth, resilience and leadership in their respective careers has been truly inspirational.' At the time of writing, Michael very proudly points out that 'collectively our family now has over 100 years of service in various elements of the ADF.'

Among Michael's proudest moments was being able to serve on deployment in the Middle East Area of Operations with both Tara and Jason, all at the same time – 'to be deployed in an operational environment, and linked with each other, remains something that we will always treasure.'

Looking back, Michael admitted he loved his time and would highly recommend a career in today's Air Force. 'I have travelled and experienced things that I would not have been able to achieve had I have not joined, not to mention the life-long mates I have made – it has been wonderful.'

Michael pointed out that 'our mob has been defending country for over 60,000 years, it is part of our DNA and is something that we will always continue to do.'

Above: Warrant Officer Michael Enchong briefing students. (Michael Enchong)

WALTER GRAHAM ELLIOT MCDONALD

Service Number:	41485
Date of Birth:	20 April 1923
Place of Birth:	Colac, Victoria
Date of Enlistment:	25 June 1941
Place of Enlistment:	Melbourne, Victoria
Date of Discharge:	24 January 1946
Rank:	Corporal
Campaign:	Second World War

Walter was born in Colac, Victoria, on 20 April 1923. In May 1941, just days after turning 18, he applied to join the RAAF at No 1 Recruiting Centre in Melbourne. On 28 May, he underwent a trade test and interview and was assessed as young, keen and alert but with limited experience as a clerk. He was therefore invited to enlist as an Office Orderly rather than in the more demanding Clerk General mustering. Returning to the Recruiting Centre on 25 June, Walter enlisted as an Aircraftman Class 1 Office Orderly for the duration of the war plus 12 months.

Initially posted to No 1 Wireless Air Gunners School in Ballarat, on 20 July Walter reported to the Signals School at RAAF Point Cook where he successfully completed No 21 Office Orderlies Course on 28 July. He then commenced duty at Air Force Headquarters in Melbourne on 5 August. Following several months of work experience, Walter re-mustered to Clerk Signals on 2 February 1942 and, on 4 March, was posted to the Melbourne Wireless Transmitting Station located at Victoria Barracks. The station had formed in February 1942 as a separate unit, having previously been a section of the Air Force Headquarters Directorate of Signals. With 357 personnel on strength in March 1942, and with signals traffic in the millions per month, the Melbourne Wireless Transmitting Station encompassed several subordinate sections including a Signals Cypher section, transmitting stations at Laverton and Point Cook, and remote sensing centres at Mont Park and Werribee.

Above: Ventilation was of paramount importance in the hot and sticky climate. Clerks are wearing shorts, boots and ID tags at a minimum. (State Library Victoria, Argus Collection)

Opposite: Formal portrait of Walter McDonald. (Australian War Memorial)

Walter was reclassified to leading aircraftman on 1 June 1942 and promoted to corporal on 1 December. He was then posted to No 14 Fighter Control Sector Headquarters on 23 May 1943. This unit was formed at Camden, New South Wales, on 23 May 1943 under the command of Wing Commander Gordon H. Steege, an RAAF fighter ace who had previously seen distinguished service in the Middle East. The unit was a forerunner of the current No 114 Mobile Control and Reporting Unit based at Darwin in the Northern Territory. At the time No 14 Fighter Control Sector, later designated Mobile, was formed, the RAAF had the job of attacking enemy forward bases in Timor, New Britain and the Solomon Islands.

On 16 June 1943, less than a month after it was formed, Walter was among No 14 (Mobile) Fighter Control Sector's 16 officers and 250 other ranks who disembarked at Goodenough Island in the Solomon Sea. Equipped with the Light Weight Air Warning Mk.I and Mk.II radars, the unit became operational on 27 June. At Goodenough Island, codenamed *Ginger* by the Allies, No 14 Fighter Control Sector formed part of No 71 Wing. The 80th Fighter Squadron USAAF allotted two P-38 Lightnings on stand-by, from dawn to dusk, to intercept enemy reconnaissance aircraft and No 79 Squadron RAAF placed two Spitfires on stand-by for intercepting enemy aircraft over the air base. The first alert was called on 1 July, when an enemy 'Dinah' (Mitsubishi Ki-46) was reported to be approaching Goodenough Island. On 13 August, the unit completed its

Left: RAAF ground staff were among the first to land on Los Negros Island in the Admiralty Islands. The image shows airmen, camped in foxholes in a bomb-blasted coconut plantation, hanging out their blankets and other items to dry. (State Library Victoria, Argus Collection)

Right: RAAF recruits prepare bed rolls and sweep barracks ready for inspection. (Mitchell Library, State Library of New South Wales)

move to Kiriwina, the largest of the Trobriand Islands, from where it supported Allied efforts to capture Rabaul on New Ireland. Its role was to warn of approaching enemy aircraft, assist in the location of downed Allied aircraft and aircrew, and also to report the movement of storm fronts to the meteorologists.

The unit was renamed No 114 (Mobile) Fighter Sector on 18 October 1943. The change was administrative and did not affect operations. The Kittyhawks of No 78 Squadron arrived at Kiriwina on 16 November, becoming the third fighter squadron controlled by No 114 (Mobile) Fighter Sector Headquarters. Operations ceased at Kiriwina on 28 February 1944 and the unit moved to Los Negros, one of the Admiralty Islands, arriving there with No 73 Wing on 16 March and commencing operations on 2 April. On Los Negros, No 114 (Mobile) Fighter Control Sector Headquarters exercised operational control of five radar stations located in the Admiralty Islands: No 337 (Momote Airfield), 340 (Bat Island and, later, Aitape), 345 (Bipi Island and, later, Harengan Island), 346 (Bundralis Mission), and 347 (Moakareng plantation). In May alone, it recorded 1,117 sorties flown. Allied formations of between 20 and 40 aircraft were striking targets from Biak in the west to Guam and Truk in the north. In the succeeding months, the unit supported the U.S. Seventh Fleet and the Thirteenth Air Force as they proceeded to strike Palau, Koror and the Malakai Islands. By August, following the move forward of the Thirteenth Air Force, operational activity declined markedly, although, from a radar perspective, it continued to be a very busy time as more than 22,000 reports were received in August from four radar stations.

Walter departed No 114 (Mobile) Fighter Control Sector Headquarters on posting back to Australia, disembarking in Brisbane on 6 September 1944. He reported to No 1 Personnel Depot in Melbourne on 20 September and from there to No 2 Personnel Depot at Bradfield Park in Sydney on 30 October. On 27 December, he embarked for overseas service again, this time in Townsville, headed for Madang, New Guinea, to take up a posting at Madang Wireless Transmitting Station. Australian troops entered Madang on 24 April 1944 after nearly three months of fighting alongside American forces. After liberating the town, Australian soldiers advanced along the North Coast Road towards Alexishafen. Madang had been heavily bombed by the Allied air forces with most of its buildings in ruins. Once it was repaired, it became an Australian Army headquarters and a base area for the remainder of the war. Walter stayed in Madang until well after the cessation of hostilities on 15 August 1945. He disembarked in Cairns on 29 December, transiting through No 1 Reserve Personnel Pool in Townsville before proceeding to No 1 Personnel Depot on 8 January for discharge.

Corporal Walter McDonald discharged from the RAAF in Melbourne on 24 January 1946.

PATRICIA THOMPSON

Date of Birth:	17 February 1971
Place of Birth:	Cunnamulla, Queensland
Date of Enlistment:	28 June 2019
Place of Enlistment:	Adelaide, South Australia
Rank:	Squadron Leader

As Paul Kelly tells us – 'from little things big things grow'. I strongly believe it is time for sharing our culture, forgiveness and, most of all, equality for all Australians.

I was born in Cunnamulla, western Queensland, in 1971. I am a proud descendant of the Mardigan and Kooma tribe in south-west Queensland. Graduating from Cunnamulla State School in 1988, I started my working life as a health worker/educator with Queensland Health and community-controlled organisations throughout the state.

In 2009, I graduated from Deakin University, Geelong, with a Bachelor of Education (Primary). I then gained employment with the Queensland Department of Education and the Abu Dhabi Education Council in the United Arab Emirates, embarking on a ten-year teaching career.

I joined the Royal Australian Air Force as an officer in June 2019. Initial officer training took me through to December 2019 and I then took up my first posting: Indigenous Liaison Officer (ILO), No 17 Squadron, RAAF Base Tindal. In 2022, I was fortunate to be able to assume the role of Senior Indigenous Liaison Officer, working out of Air Command on the edge of the Blue Mountains in Glenbrook.

During my time at Tindal, I worked hard to strengthen the ongoing relationship between Air Force and the Indigenous Language Groups within the Katherine region through meaningful engagement and dialogue. The key to reconciliation is bringing Aboriginal and Torres Strait Islander and non-Indigenous Australians together as one.

Opposite: Royal Australian Air Force Indigenous Liason Officer Flight Lieutenant Patricia Thompson, with her mother, Jessie Collins, and sister, Anne Wharton, holding the Air Force newspaper she appears in, at Charleville Airport. (RAAF)

While I was with No 17 Squadron, I was involved in Exercise *Christmas Hop* with No 35 Squadron's C-27J Spartan aircraft. We delivered supplies to remote Aboriginal and Torres Strait Islander communities in far north Queensland, just in time for the holiday season. Organisations from across Australia were actively involved in donating such items as school supplies, sporting equipment, first aid kits and toiletries. It remains one of the most memorable and rewarding moments of my Air Force career so far.

In my new role as Senior Indigenous Liaison Officer, I will continue to work hard with my ILO network positioned at various bases across Australia. I strongly believe it is time for sharing our culture, forgiveness and, most of all, equality for all Australians. Reconciliation is also a time for healing and we can do this by having respectful, honest conversations to enable us to work together and restore what has been broken.

As Paul Kelly tells us – 'from little things big things grow'.

Above: Warrant Officer of the Air Force, Warrant Officer Fiona Grasby OAM, and Indigenous Liaison Officer for RAAF Base Tindal, Flight Lieutenant Patricia Thompson (left), with a plaque commemorating the opening of the RAAF Base Tindal Yarning Circle. (RAAF)

Opposite: Indigenous Liaison Officer for RAAF Base Tindal, Flight Lieutenant Patricia Thompson, takes a photo of some local children in front of an F/A-18B Hornet at the Jericho Jarli launch at RAAF Base Tindal. (RAAF)

PHILOMENA DAVID

Date of Birth:	15 December 1952
Place of Birth:	Thursday Island, Torres Strait, Queensland
Date of Enlistment:	29 June 1971
Place of Enlistment:	Townsville
Date of Discharge:	29 June 1991
Rank:	Flight Sergeant

I decided on a whim to attend the interview and the rest is history.

Philomena David is a proud Kulkalgal woman from Iama (Yam) Island from the Central Cluster group of the Torres Strait. Her family totem is the Dog Clan (Umai).

Philomena was raised on Hammond Island, one of the near island groups, close to Thursday Island, where all the Government Administration was conducted. 'Back then, Hammond was predominately occupied by Catholics, so I ended up attending Our Lady of the Sacred Heart School, on Hammond, then later travelled daily in a school barge, attending the High School on Thursday Island.'

'I finally finished my secondary education at Mount St Bernard College, at Herberton, on the Atherton Tablelands in Queensland, where my fondest memories whilst growing up, were attending family outings, ceremonial feastings, and Cultural Practices, also listening to stories told to us by our Elders.'

While it was not planned, Philomena was so impressed with a visit from RAAF Recruiters, she made her mind up to apply for entry into the RAAF and enlisted shortly thereafter on 29 June 1971. 'I decided on a whim to attend the interview and the rest is history.'

Philomena completed recruit training before moving to RAAF Base Wagga to undertake specialist Supplier trade training, seeing her first posting to RAAF Base Amberley in Queensland. However, Philomena changed paths during her career and spent time as a Drill Instructor teaching new female recruits about Service life and the expectations of drill and parades, discipline, conduct, and dress and bearing. This would see her serve in various locations including Queensland, Victoria and South Australia. After promotion to sergeant, Philomena transferred roles again, becoming a Service Policewoman at RAAF Bases Darwin and Fairbairn, Canberra, before promotion to flight sergeant, a move to RAAF Base Williamtown near Newcastle and her final posting before discharging after a very busy and successful 20-year career on 29 June 1991.

Left: Aircraftwoman Philomena David. (Philomena David)

Talking about her initial aspirations, 'My mother, God rest her soul, was the driving force behind me, to leave the island way of life, and to travel and experience bigger and better things, that she could only imagine. She told me later that she always knew I would do well and was very proud every time I would return home on leave. I did this for my family, my people and to serve my country.'

'Here I was, enlisted in the Royal Australian Air Force, serving my country, and making my family proud; to me, that was my greatest achievement. Only years after, when I think back on my years served, I would smile and reflect on my mother's words: "Always be kind and show respect to your Elders and peers, stand firm on whatever decision you make and honour that, wherever you go on this life's journey." As an Indigenous woman, I am extremely proud that I'm one of many that was not afraid to enlist, despite all odds, and came out with flying colours. I'm so grateful for the recognition. Those were the happiest and most memorable times that I will always treasure. We walk this great land together, side by side as Australians, irrespective of one's colour or creed and respect goes both ways; after all, we are Australians.'

Those were the happiest and most memorable times that I will always treasure."

Right: Aircraftwoman Philomena David. (Philomena David)